THREE
IN
ONE

THREE
IN
ONE

From Darkness to Light

LEAH BICKEL AND
CHRISTINA DELLA NEBBIA-AREVALO, PH.D

XULON PRESS ELITE

Xulon Press Elite
2301 Lucien Way #415
Maitland, FL 32751
407.339.4217
www.xulonpress.com

Paperback ISBN-13: 978-1-6628-2099-1
Ebook ISBN-13: 978-1-6628-2100-4

This book is a memorial dedication to Cathy, loving wife, mother, and grandmother. May her spirit from heaven bless each person reading this book.

Table of Contents

Preface

This is a book about the tremendous, everlasting, and amazing love of God, our heavenly Father has for us, His children. It is also about Jesus Christ, our Lord and Savior, who is present for us and died on the Cross for our sins so we could be reconciled with God. To Jesus we owe gratitude, love, obedience, and praise. Jesus gave us lessons of love, mercy, and forgiveness through the demonstration of His life, and through the words in scripture often delivered in parables. The book is based on Christian principles coming forth to us through scripture, prayer, and quietly listening to words from God through the Holy Spirit.

> "For God so loved the world, that He gave His only begotten Son, that whoever believes in Him shall not perish, but have eternal life." (John 3:16)

> "Now God has revealed these things to us by the Spirit, for the Spirit searches everything, even the depths of God." (1 Cor. 2:10)

This book is about the power of prayer and how God listens to each prayer we send up to Him. We may not always get the answer we are looking for or get our prayers answered right away. God has His way of always answering prayers perfectly and in the right time. That means that we must wait patiently on the Lord for the answer. While waiting, praise will be on our lips at all times. We must trust that He is the almighty one, and He is in control.

> "I will praise the Lord at all times and His praise is always on my lips." (Psalm. 31:1)

In God's infinite and perfect mind, He knows and answers our prayers in the way that is best for us. He listens and answers and always gives us what we need. He is not a genie in a bottle but a living, real God who gives us good things when we ask Him. Sometimes, we must suffer and offer up that suffering for God, always praising Him in good times and in bad times. Remember, we are not God, and we must trust Him when we pray. Through our circumstances, which are sometimes unpleasant, we learn to grow closer to God and learn valuable lessons that help us grow spiritually. Eventually, He will answer our prayers perfectly every time.

Although this book contains real events about His love and healing, not everyone who asks for a healing receives it. Nothing passes through this earth that does not pass by God first. God is in control. Therefore, if we trust in God and Jesus, knowing that the way He answers prayers is perfect for us, we learn to depend upon Him and do His will with a humble spirit.

The urging of God came upon Christina and Leah in the fall of 2019 to write this book. Although they both felt the gentle nudge to complete a book about their experiences, they did not start writing this book until December of that year. At that time, God was relentless, and they both felt that God placed the importance of writing this book immediately. It was then that the work began in earnest, and the final details and revisions took place during the onset of the coronavirus (COVID-19) in March 2020. Christina felt the need to turn to God in praise during those trying times. It was through prayer and reflection that she focused on what was important: relationships, loving each other and God, and always trusting Him. Leah was also receiving the gentle but persistent message from God that this book must be completed now, at this time.

This book is a message of hope. It is a message of the power of God and how He loves us and can heal us if we ask Him. Although the testimonies and experiences of each of the authors can be backed up with medical evidence, it is not the intention to do so. Rather, this book contains the true testimonies of the power of turning toward God in praise, thanksgiving, and trust that He is always with us and will never turn away. His beloved son Jesus Christ is always with us and guides our steps, along with the Holy Spirit.

Leah and Christina both practice their faith as Catholics. They also identify with the Catholic charismatic movement and belong to a prayer group that uses the gifts of the Holy

Spirit that were given to each member of the group by God. The group meets in a Catholic Church, and in coordination with the priest, the group members offer healing prayers after mass for those who ask for it.

It is our desire, that even in these difficult times of social distancing during COVID-19 that we can become closer to God, understanding and trusting Him rather than panicking, hoarding food, and other items, and looking out for only ourselves. Rather, it is a time to *praise Him* for every circumstance, give to the less fortunate, and show love to our neighbors. Prayer is also important, and it can change things.

Blessings to all that are reading this book and are always trusting in Jesus. These difficult times are temporary, but may we learn the lessons that God is teaching us now and allow ourselves to humbly do His will now and forever.

Note: This book is based on the perspectives of each author. Some of the names and identifying information has been changed to preserve the anonymity of certain individuals. However, the events described are based on real events.

"Trust in the LORD forever, for in the LORD GOD you have an everlasting rock." (Isa. 26:4).

Deuteronomy 31:8
"The Lord himself goes before you and will be with you; he will never leave you nor forsake you. Do not be afraid; do not be discouraged".

Isaiah 55:11
"So is my word that goes out from my mouth: It will not return to me empty, but will accomplish what I desire and achieve the purpose for which I sent it".

You are never alone—Jesus is just a whispered prayer away.

The Beginning
of a Friendship,
Told by Leah

The beginning of a friendship between Christina and me started at a charismatic prayer meeting at the church we both attended. The first time I saw Christina was when she walked into the prayer meeting. She looked like she felt out of place and a little lost. We all introduced ourselves, and I tried to give her a warm welcome. I was not sure she would return to the next meeting. The second time we met, a true friendship started. It felt as if we knew each other a lifetime, yet we had just met. There was a mingling of our spirits and a friendship that probably started in heaven before we came to earth. The friendship was orchestrated all through God's hands.

A charismatic prayer meeting is a way to worship Jesus in prayer and song through the Holy Spirit. We acknowledge the presence of God the Father, Jesus the Christ, and the Holy Spirit as the disciples did in Acts chapter 2 when the Holy Spirit descended upon all the people in the upper room. The charismatic group of which we belonged set up prayer teams after different masses so we could pray for the needs of the people of the parish. It was announced before mass began that prayer teams would be available after mass.

Our prayer teams offered to pray for emotional, spiritual, or physical healing for the individual him/herself, another family member, or a friend. Thus, we walked in the power of the Spirit by faith. Jesus said He must go so He could send the Holy Spirit as an advocate for us. We trusted that God the Father, Jesus Christ, and the Holy Spirit would make us the instruments through which They would use to heal various individuals who approached us after mass for healing prayer.

> "But very truly I tell you, it is for your good that I am going away. Unless I go away, the Advocate will not come to you; but if I go, I will send him to you. When he comes, he will prove the world to be wrong about sin and righteous and judgement." (John 16:7–8)

The Holy Spirit is the dispenser of the gifts or charisms of God. In scripture the gifts are listed in the book of Isaiah.

> "The Spirit of the Lord will rest on him. The spirit of wisdom understanding, the spirit of counsel and of might, the spirit of the knowledge and of fear of the Lord and he will delight in the fear

of the Lord. He will not judge by what he sees with his eyes or decide what he hears with his ears." (Isa. 11:2–3)

These are called the Isaiah gifts. The gifts St. Paul speaks of are found in First Corinthians:

"Now you are the body of Christ, and each one of you are a part of it. And God has placed in the church first of all apostles, second prophets, third teachers, then miracles, then gifts of healing, of helping, of guidance, and different kinds of tongues. Are all apostles? Are all prophets? Are all teachers? Do all work miracles? Do all have gifts of healing? Do all speak in tongues? Do all interpret? Now eagerly desire the greater gifts." (1 Cor. 12:27–31)

At the church we attended, the prayer group offered a "Life in the Spirit" seminar. I volunteered to be a group leader for the ladies. Christina was assigned to my group, and I became her sponsor. The fourth week of the seminar, I take those I sponsor out to dinner to answer any questions and discuss how the seminar has impacted their lives. I also ask them to be in fervent prayer before the next meeting. That meeting is when we pray for the release of the Holy Spirit upon those who request it, to dispense His gifts for them, and to work through them. This is a powerful time of faith and action. Many times, the Holy Spirit will make known the gift He is giving them to the person being prayed for.

Before the dinner, I was in fervent prayer for the ladies I was sponsoring. I was asking for guidance for the discussion we were going to have at dinner. During prayer and a listening session, the Holy Spirit told me the gifts He was going to release to each of the ladies I sponsored. This was the first time this disclosure happened, and I was overwhelmed but also excited. Our dinner was powerful, and I could feel the presence of God throughout the whole meal. I did not reveal to the women what the Holy Spirit said about the gifts He was giving them. I did tell them that I was aware of what gifts each of them was going to receive. I felt I was to pray for them to have a powerful encounter with the Holy Spirit. This seminar transformed the friendship between Christina and me to sisters in Christ.

Christina and I have become close friends. We stay in contact with each other several times per week. Although we live in separate towns, we often pray for each other, talk about various topics, and help each other out when needed. Our friendship is indeed a gift from God, and we both cherish our relationship and how it helps us grow closer in spirit to God the Father, the Son, and the Holy Spirit.

Leah's Testimony

I n May of 2017, my husband said he planned to retire later that year. I was already retired as a nurse and later as a small business owner. We lived in the Dallas–Fort Worth metroplex area. I started praying and asking the Lord whether we should stay in Texas or move home to Mississippi. It felt the Lord wanted us to go to Mississippi, and I felt Him say "Go home; your family needs you."

> "My sheep hear my voice, and I know them, and they follow Me. And I give them eternal life, and they never perish; neither shell any one snatch them out of my hand." (John 10:27-28)

In September of 2017, we moved home to Mississippi where my family lived. My husband and I had to start all over again. We had to find a church, new physicians, a new bank, and plenty of new things that one needs to find when moving to a new area. The time flew as we got settled in, and it was way past time for my yearly physical. So, after finding a new health clinic in late October of 2018, I finally had a health screening and a mammogram, two months later than usual. Three weeks later in early November, I found out that something suspicious had been found on my mammogram and that I needed to come back for a more involved diagnostic mammogram.

I was not too concerned because I had been called back to repeat a mammogram a few times. I scheduled a diagnostic mammogram and ultrasound for the end of November. At the end of the ultrasound, I was told they believed that I had breast cancer that would need to be biopsied. I felt alarmed. Now I was concerned, but prayer on the way home brought me peace.

> "Therefore having been justified by faith, we have peace with God through our Lord Jesus Christ." (Rom. 5:1)

The medical personnel scheduled a biopsy to be performed on my affected breast. I arrived at the office where the biopsy was performed. A marker was inserted where the abnormal cells were in the breast, and some tissue was removed. The doctor who was performing the procedure said, "It does not look benign, and I don't want to give you false hope." We would not know for sure about the outcome until the biopsy report came back. I walked out of that office filled with dread. I called out to the Lord saying, "Please, God, don't let me have cancer." I walked around for a week in a daze, crying out to God begging him to not let this be cancer.

On December 7, 2018, the health clinic called and said the biopsy report was ready, but they would not give me any information over the phone. I scheduled a face-to-face appointment for the results. When I arrived at the clinic, I was not in a state of grace; I was a basket case. I felt overwhelmed with emotion. The physician looked at the papers and told me the dreaded results. The report stated I had invasive ductal carcinoma. I have never felt so alone, and I was in the darkest place in my life.

> "The Lord himself goes before you and will be with you; he will never leave you or forsake you. Do not be afraid; do not be discouraged." (Deut. 31:8) NIV

The health clinic made an appointment with an oncologist at the cancer clinic for December 12, 2018. They took care of the details and chose the oncologist for me. God's hand was moving, but I did not recognize it. When I got home, I was so devastated I could not even pray. I have never felt so hopeless and full of fear in my life.

"Fear not, for I am with you;
 Be not dismayed, for I am your God.
 I will strengthen you,
 Yes, I will help you,
 I will uphold you with My righteous
 right hand."

(Isa. 41:10)

I just kept repeating, "I don't understand God; I just don't understand!" At this point, I could not even ask for prayers from others. In asking, I had to come to grips that I had cancer, and I just did not understand why. Since I was still in such an intense emotional state, I could not even form the words to tell the rest of my family and friends. I felt so alone—where was my God, my Abba?

> "Now He who searches the hearts knows what the mind of the Spirit is, because He makes intersession for the saints according to the will of God. And we know that all things work together for the good of those who are called according to his purpose." (Rom. 8:27-28)

On December 7, 2018, I knew I needed to text my sisters in Christ. These beautiful ladies are powerful prayer warriors, and they needed to know I needed prayer. There are seven of us in this prayer group, and each one walks in the gifts of the Holy Spirit. Also, I had to tell my daughter that I had cancer. My husband and I had just returned home after being away for seventeen years. She took it better than I did. She said " Mom, God has got this. Prayer works." I felt relieved in those words that she spoke to me.

> "Now you are the body of Christ, and member individually and God has

appointed these in the church: first apostles, second prophets, third teachers, after that miracles, then gifts of healing, helps administrations, varieties of tongues. But be earnestly and desire the best gifts. And yet I show you a more excellent way." (1Cor. 12: 27-31)

Those beautiful prayer warriors have a personal relationship with God. He speaks to them, and they hear His voice. Sometimes He whispers, and other times He speaks to them through scripture and other people. All these ladies sit down and spend time with God, seeking His face and His words. They walk with Him daily. They call out to Him and rest in His love.

That same heartbreaking day, I sat down and wrote the hardest text of my life. I wrote, "Ladies, I need your prayers. I have been diagnosed with breast cancer. I have an appointment to see the oncologist on December 12, 2018." Within thirty minutes my phone blew up like a Christmas tree. Here are some of the prayers said on my behalf:

"Now, let us all get in agreement in prayer, to ask that the cancer is going to be in one spot only. They are going to remove that little spot, leaving nothing behind. Let us thank Him together for His healing and His protection over our sister Leah."

"We come together agreeing that He is going to keep moving in a mighty way on Leah's behalf. Bring total healing and restoration to her body. This we pray in Jesus's name. Amen."

> "For where two or three are gathered in My name, I am there in the midst of them." (Matt. 18:20)

"Let us not become weary in doing good, for at the proper time we will reap a harvest if we do not give up." (Gal. 6:9)

Another wrote: "Faith the size of a mustard seed can move mountains. Let our joined faith grow that mustard seed into the healing power that will move the mountain called cancer out of Sister Leah's body. We offer up Leah to our Lord and Savior Jesus Christ for healing and recovery. Hallelujah, and be healed. Amen."

Another sweet prayer warrior wrote: "Leah, there is confirmation about what God put in my Spirit the day we spoke. Our prayers can move mountains. All is well, my sweet sister."

> "Because of your unbelief; for assuredly, I say to you, if you have the faith as a mustard seed, you will say to this mountain, move from here to there, and it will move; and nothing will be impossible for you." (Matt. 17:20)

These are just some of the many prayers spoken for me. There were so many more. I had the support of my family and my sisters and brothers in Christ. All these prayers gave me the courage to trust in my Savior Jesus Christ. Where there had been hopelessness, I now had hope and my faith was renewed.

> "Now faith is the substance of things hoped for, the evidence of things not seen." (Heb. 11:1)

I called Christina on December 10, three days later, and asked her to sit down and have a listening session with the Lord. I asked her to storm the heavens in prayer about my circumstance. She prayed with me over the phone and then had a listening session with the Lord. This is what she emailed me.

These are the words that the Lord spoke to her:

My Child,

Leah is one of my chosen ones, and I have her in the palm of my hand. You asked why I gave her cancer. Why did you have cancer? You must understand that I can take a difficult situation and have good come from it. You must trust and pray for her with mighty prayers. The enemy is threatened by her faithfulness. I will not let the enemy defeat Me. Remember nothing happens that does not pass by Me first. You will see the fruits of your prayers. Come together and pray with your friends and sisters in Christ for her. Pray the novena to the Sacred Heart of Jesus every day as you did for yourself when you had cancer and others when interventions were needed. This will be a trial by fire, and it is something she must go through,

but she will come back stronger. Have
peace, my child, and send her peace
and prayers, prayers, plenty of prayers.
I AM is surrounding her with a blanket
of love and protection. Send your love
to her through your mind and with your
voice. Love can heal. My love and hand
can and *will* heal.

—I AM.

Upon reading this, I cried out to the Lord. I am not Job. Lord, I do not even like to read the book of Job in the Bible! I continued to pray for healing, and I felt the Lord's love.

On December 12, 2018, I went to the cancer clinic to see the oncologist. When my husband and I walked in the door, the place was packed. We could hardly find a seat. I looked around and was amazed at the number of people who were there and had cancer. Cancer does not care who you are. There were people there from every walk of life and every nationality.

The oncologist was an amazing person. She put me at ease and gave me hope. We discussed what type of surgery was needed, and she explained the biopsy report. The reported stated I had invasive ductal carcinoma stage 1, measuring 4 mm in length. It was tiny. For the first time in weeks, I had peace. She told me to schedule an appointment with the surgeon at the desk on the way out. When checking out, my hope was dashed when I was told the only appointment I could have was January 8, 2019. Cancer does not wait for doctors to become available; it continues to grow. While my husband and I were talking, the oncologist called the front desk and said she had talked to the surgeon and had booked an appointment for me on December 17, 2018. God's hand had moved.

When I met with the surgeon on December 17, he explained the cancer was so small he recommended a lumpectomy. He then took me to the desk of the person who scheduled all the surgeries. The earliest they could get me on the surgery schedule was January 3, 2019. I told her if there were any cancellations to please call me. I would be available for the earliest surgery opening. I went home and called all my prayer warriors and sent out emails and said I know God's hand will move. Please pray I can have surgery sooner that January 3. The next day the surgery center called and said they had a cancellation, and I could come in the next day, December 19, 2018. Surgery was scheduled for 11:00 a.m. The nurse told me to be at the clinic for a mammogram at 7:00 a.m. to get ready for my surgery. I was excited but a little anxious, but so grateful to God that the surgery was moved up so I could put a stop to the cancer and be rid of it once and for all.

One day when I was in deep prayer with the Lord, I heard His voice tell me to place my hand upon my affected breast. I did as He asked, and my hand became warm and then as hot as an iron. I felt an intense heat that radiated through my body. I also felt an incredible peace.

On the day of surgery, the surgeon performed a mammogram to check on the marker that was placed in my breast in order to show where the cancer was in the original biopsy and then read the mammogram. The surgeon came back smiling. He did not know what had happened, but there was no sign of cancer at all—it was completely gone! He said the biopsy must have gotten rid of all the cancer. Surgery was still needed to see if any lymph nodes were involved and to make sure the cancer had not spread. The marker also needed to be removed. I thought I had a miracle. I left that room praising God.

The surgery was performed. I had an easy recovery. I was scheduled for a post-operative check on January 3, 2019, the day of the original scheduled surgery. Those two weeks were spent in fervent prayer asking, "God, please, no chemo. Please do not let it be necessary." So, on January 3, 2019, I met with the surgeon and went over the biopsy report from the surgery that stated there was cancer, and it was 5 mm at the greatest dimension, and still at stage one. There was no lymph node involvement.

I asked," What do we do now?" Even though I knew that God had healed me, I am not so sure the doctor felt the same way. Doctors make their decisions based on facts, tests, and empirical evidence. The doctor did not know what to do with me because I was an enigma. The cancer was seen on the first biopsy report, but there was no sign of it on the mammogram right before my surgery. The surgeon said my case would be presented to the tumor board, a group of physicians who were cancer experts. My oncologist would make the final decision about treatment after consulting with the tumor board.

On January 10, 2019, I met with the oncologist to discuss what manner of treatment was indicated. She told me the tumor board had met that morning, and my case was discussed. She said, "I have decided no chemo. I will not put you through that." I was so excited I wanted to jump up and down, do a happy dance, fist bump my doctor, and yell, "You go, God." Being a mature grandmother, I said instead, "What do you recommend?" She answered," You will have five days of radiation." My prayers were answered.

On January 17, 2019, I met with the surgeon and a catheter was inserted into the cavity where the tumor was located. This allowed the catheter to deliver an individual dose of radiation, so my physician could customize my treatment. This is called a SAVI. One must meet special criteria, and I did meet it.

On January 18, 2019, I went to the radiation lab and had a cat scan to see if the catheter was in the correct place. Then I met with the radiologist, and we discussed the procedure. I had to come twice a day and have a radiation treatment. Each treatment would last about three minutes. I started radiation therapy on January 21, 2019. The third day of treatment, the technician said to me, "You are always so cheerful. You must have a great support group."

I said, "Yes, I do." I thought to myself, I have my husband, family, and prayer warriors in several states praying for me. I have all the angels and saints in heaven cheering me on, and Jesus holding my hand as I walk through this time of need. I am not alone, and I am blessed.

> "Confess your trespasses to one another, and pray for one another, that you may be healed. The effective, fervent prayer of a righteous man avails much." (James 5:16)

> "What then shall we say to these things? If God is for us who can be against us?" (Rom. 8:31)

On January 25, 2019, I walked into the waiting room after the last treatment. I was cancer free! I walked over to my husband, and God spoke and said, "See that woman over there? Go and pray for her." My husband and I both went to her. I do not know her name, but I still pray for her because I know what it is to feel hopeless.

I wanted my healing to be a miracle. I wanted to be healed instantly. Instead, my healing was a divine process, orchestrated by God's power, and executed by all the doctors, nurses, and health professionals I was blessed with. Only God can turn a mess into a message. What was my message? Trust Me.

Only God can turn a test into a testimony. Walking through the treatment of cancer holding God's hand is my testimony. Only God can turn a trial into a triumph; I triumphed over cancer and fear by God's hand of divine mercy.

Only God can turn a victim into victory. I was a victim of cancer; now I walk in victory by God's love and divine healing power.

A few months later, God spoke and said, "Child, you did not leave Me."

I said, " Lord, where would I go? You are my God, Savior, and Friend. I had a choice, and I chose You." When you go through a trial, who will you choose? Everything in life is a choice.

"Like newborn babes, long for the pure spiritual milk which is without guile, that ye may grow thereby unto salvation; if ye have tasted that the Lord is gracious." (1 Pet. 2:2–3)

A Conversation Between God and Leah

October 2020

"Child, it has been two years since you were diagnosed with cancer. You have walked through the fire and now shine like burnished gold. You have prayed for many people. When they came to you for prayer before your cancer diagnosis, did you see their anguish?"

"No, God, I did not."

God spoke, "I looked deep into their heart and saw great sorrow."

"Child, did you feel their pain?"

"No, God, I did not."

"The Great I Am felt their pain, and I was moved. They came to Me for prayer and called on my Name. Child, did you see their brokenness?"

"No, God, I did not."

"Child do you remember when I spoke and said what is broken can be fixed?"

"Yes, God, I do."

"That is when I touch them. I took the broken lives and minds and restored them. Child did you see their hopelessness?"

"No, God, I did not."

"I did, and I gave them hope. Child, did you understand when they came for prayer that they had humbled themselves? They were crying out to Me."

"No, God, I did not."

"I looked deep into their spirits and restored their souls and claimed them for Myself. They were calling out for My Son Jesus. He made them worthy by His death and resurrection. He is My Son, the shepherd of My flock. He cares for each of My own. Child, when you pray for people now, do you see My hand move?"

"Yes, Lord, I do. I now feel Your love as You surround us. I hear Your voice as You give the message to be spoken. I feel Your power as You heal their bodies. I see the joy in their faces as they feel Your touch and love for them. I see the radiance on their faces as they let go of their despair and hopelessness, and I see Your love surround them."

Several months ago, on January 1, 2020, God spoke and said to me,

> "From my heart to your heart
> From my thoughts to your lips
> From my Spirit to your spirit
> My grace to you,
> Shalom."

Christina's Testimony

The Diagnosis

I walked briskly from the parking lot to the hospital with my mother to get the long-awaited colonoscopy completed. It was June 2014, and the weather was relentlessly hot as is usual for north-central Texas. The hospital was in a northern suburb of the Dallas–Fort Worth metroplex and was a well-respected hospital. My emotions were numb, but I noticed the heat that radiated from the parking lot while I walked with my mother to the reception area of the hospital.

Since I was undergoing general anesthesia, my eighty-one-year-old mother accompanied me to give me moral support and drive me home after the procedure was completed. I was not fearful of the colonoscopy procedure but did notice some gastrointestinal symptoms that were somewhat bothersome over the past year. It was my style to shrug off minor physical complaints and work hard at my practice as a psychologist. I felt it was my mission to help others, even at the cost of sacrificing my own health. My primary care physician recommended that I obtain a colonoscopy when I turned fifty, but I simply put it off and viewed it as unimportant. I felt as if the probability of having cancer was so remote, it was not worth my concern or my time. My patients came first, was my thinking. I soon came to regret this decision.

After registering at the hospital and taking care of the insurance and other paperwork, I was escorted to the outpatient surgery area. I changed into a hospital gown and lay on the bed, waiting for the nurse to finish her vital signs and explain what to expect. I felt so cold and vulnerable; the hospital was stark and sterile, and I felt over-exposed in the scant hospital gown. The nurse was kind and offered me a warm blanket, which helped me feel more comfortable. I felt comfort from my mother's presence, as she has always been there for me throughout my entire life.

I had a short talk with the anesthesiologist about the medication that was to be used for the procedure. I had experienced complications from anesthesia twice before when I had my tonsils removed in my early twenties and again when I had a D and C from a miscarriage when I was married. The anesthesiologist was a young physician and seemed perfectly comfortable while explaining the procedure and medications he was going to use. I was happy to learn that there were advancements made in the medications used for anesthesia, and I was able to get all my questions answered. As I laid in the bed waiting for the procedure to begin, my mind reminisced of my divorce that occurred five years prior to this point in time. It was all a blur to me now, but I realized how much I had loved my ex-husband, despite the problems we had that led to divorce.

I longed for his presence beside my bed even though we were divorced.

I dealt with the pain of my divorce by dating a lot of men to distract me. I was looking for a quick fix for my pain and did not make the right decisions because it did not heal me emotionally; it just numbed the pain. I was still a practicing Catholic woman who went to mass on Sundays. However, my lifestyle was not consistent with church teaching. I used casual encounters with various men to comfort myself, then compartmentalized my behavior when I went to work or church. God had something in mind for me to address this issue, but I had no idea at the time what I would have to go through to learn the valuable lesson God wanted me to learn.

I was grateful for the short time my mother was with me. I quickly began to pray and asked God to protect me during the procedure and for a good outcome. I remembered the verse,

> "Be not afraid for I am with you."
> (Deut. 31:8)

I imagined Jesus sitting next to me, holding my hand, and that image gave me great comfort. Perhaps that was God's plan for me—to have only Him to turn to in order to derive strength and comfort.

> "Have I not commanded you? Be strong
> and courageous. Do not be afraid; do

> not be discouraged, for the LORD your
> God will be with you wherever you go."
> (Josh. 1:9)

I realized that I had no significant partner or persons besides my family to help me now. My family lived about four hours away, and I had no one to comfort me on a daily basis. I was still suffering emotionally from the aftermath of the divorce after having been married to a man I loved deeply for twenty years and had three wonderful children with. However, the marriage ended tragically in a difficult divorce, and although I did everything I could to prevent it, the divorce went through because my husband did not want to remain married. I remembered the good times and prayed that God would send me another man to love one day, one who would help me grow spiritually if it was His will. Despite the longing I felt for my ex-husband, I felt happy and blessed that my elderly mother was still able to drive and take care of me as I waded through the paperwork and medical aspects of the procedure.

I felt a bone-chilling cold, and the hospital room appeared to be so sterile and so impersonable. Although there was a bright picture of an outdoor scene on the wall, everything else in the room appeared barren. It did little to make me feel comfortable, and I was praying that the procedure would be easy and completed quickly.

> "Show me your ways, Lord, teach me
> your paths." (Ps. 25:4)

I reminisced about my three beautiful three children who were a result of the twenty-year marriage. My children have been a great blessing from God, yet they were adults in different towns, pursuing their own lives. My thoughts were abruptly interrupted by the nurse who said it was time for the procedure. They rolled me into the operating room, and I remember thinking that it was such a small room. The nurse asked me to lie on my side. My mother was waiting patiently in the waiting room and had voiced no concerns when I left her side to the operating room. The nurse gave me an injection that she said would make me feel comfortable. Immediately after I received it, I felt like I was drunk and felt extremely relaxed. The anesthesiologist stated to me shortly after arriving in the operating room, "Are you ready to go to sleep?" I barely had time for a yes when everything turned dark.

The procedure was a quick forty-five minutes, and the next thing I knew, I was back in the recovery room with my mother by my side. I felt incredibly well, like I had just slept nine hours. Only a few minutes had passed, and the nurse told me that when I felt ready, I could sit up, sip on some juice, and get dressed. As soon as I was dressed, the anesthesiologist came back to the room as promised to see if I had any symptoms from the medications that were used during the procedure. I told him I felt great, but I felt confused because his face was so serious. He left the room quickly after I told him I felt fine.

A few minutes later, the gastroenterologist, an Indian physician, came into the room with a genuinely concerned look in her eyes. "We found cancer in your colon," the doctor stated. The room stood still when those words were announced, and I felt as if I were watching a movie. The doctor spoke again about how they would need to biopsy the tumor, but she was certain it was cancer, and I would be referred to a surgeon and oncologist for further care. I heard the words, but I felt as though I was in a vortex, and the sound of her voice was hollow. My mind became more in tune with what was being said when she showed me a photograph of the cancer tumor. It was the ugliest thing I have ever seen, with bright red, purple, and brown colors—a grotesque shape that was breaking through the wall of my colon. I was shocked and was not emotionally absorbing the medical diagnosis. I felt as though there was a chance it was not cancer because it had not yet been biopsied. I suppose I was in denial to some extent.

> "Say to those with fearful hearts, 'Be strong, do not fear; your God will come, he will come with vengeance; with divine retribution he will come to save you." (Isa. 35:4)

"Look at the birds of the air; they do not sow or reap or store away in barns, and yet your heavenly Father feeds them. Are you not much more valuable than they?" (Matt. 6:26)

The Surgery

I went home feeling very somber, and my mother attempted to reassure me. Unfortunately, she had to return to Austin where she resided, and I was on my own to navigate the next steps. After a few days, I returned to see the gastroenterologist, and it was confirmed I had cancer. I was referred to a surgeon but prayed about whether he was the right man for the job. After much prayer and consultation with my family, I was extremely fortunate to find the perfect surgeon for the job. He literally wrote the book on colon cancer surgery, and I was happy to have found the right physician for the operation.

> "If you remain in me and my words
> remain in you, ask whatever you wish,
> and it will be done for you." (John 15:7)

I scheduled my surgery at a large and reputable hospital in downtown Dallas after an office visit with the surgeon. He was a bit arrogant, but after researching his name, I realized he was by far the best physician for my type of surgery. He explained that he was going to remove my descending colon which about half of it. He would reroute the colon and stitch (anastomose) the small and large intestine together. I would have a short recovery. My body would adjust to the surgery without a colonoscopy bag. I was essentially going to have half of my colon removed, and it was going to be done laparoscopically.

Surgery was scheduled for two weeks later. I had my sister, daughter, mother, and a close friend by my side. We arrived at the hospital in downtown Dallas. That area always caused me confusion because the buildings and streets were big and overwhelming. I felt blessed to have my family and friend at my side to reassure me before and after the surgery. I remember that after I changed into a hospital gown, the surgeon came in to explain what he was going to do. I was frightened because it was major surgery, and I tried to tell myself to trust in God, that all would be well. However, my human mind did not fully grasp the meaning of trusting in God completely. When I was having my doubts, a wonderful hospital chaplain came to the side of my bed. He touched my hand and asked, "Do you want me to pray for you?" I immediately said yes, and he held my hand and prayed that God would guide the surgeon's hands and that I would have a positive outcome. After that prayer, I felt much relief and was able to focus on the love and protection I knew my God was providing me.

> "But when you ask, you must believe
> and not doubt, because the one who
> doubts is like a wave of the sea, blown
> and tossed by the wind." (James 1:6)

I remember the nurse could not get the needle into my vein and tried several times. Finally, she asked a physician to help, and he placed the needle into my vein to prepare me for surgery so medications could be delivered intravenously. A short time passed, and the nurse came to give me my pre-operation injection. It was designed to relax me, and shortly after receiving it I felt as though I was in fantasy land. Within a few minutes from the injection, I was whisked into the surgery room. I remember only a few minutes, and then I was given the drug to put me under general anesthesia. It took literally three seconds, and I was out completely.

The next thing I remember was being in the recovery room. The nurse was calling my name and trying to get me to respond. I eventually was able to talk to her, albeit with short sentences. I was still woozy from the general anesthesia, but it was quickly wearing off. I nibbled on the crackers and juice she gave me. Eventually, I was returned to my room. My mother and two sisters were at my side, and my youngest sister was a nurse. She told me that to recover as quickly as possible, it was necessary to walk around the hospital as soon as I was able to do so. I was always an overachiever, so I took those words of advice seriously and was walking around the hospital, even using stairs the very next day. I took pain medication, but I was still experiencing a lot of discomfort. I prayed for relief, but mostly for God to give me courage and resilience to forge ahead with whatever treatment was recommended as the next step.

"Be strong and courageous. Do not be afraid or terrified because of them, for the Lord your God goes with you; He

will never leave you nor forsake you."
(Deut. 31:6)

The surgeon came into my room in a very brisk manner. He told me that the surgery went well and what to expect regarding my recovery. He also stated that he had taken a biopsy of the tissue, and since the cancer had broken through the colon wall, he extracted lymph nodes that also were to be tested for cancer. I asked what that meant, and he replied that it is a more advanced stage if the lymph nodes are affected. He said that his office would call to set up the appointment for the follow-up to get my stitches out and to find out the results of the biopsy.

My sisters and mom left a few days after my surgery, and I was alone. All I had was God, and I prayed and prayed for my total and complete healing. I remember begging God to spare my life because even though my children were grown, they were in their early twenties and still needed me. I also felt that God had some things for me to do for him. I bargained with God and promised Him that if he spared my life and allowed me to live, I would turn my life over to Him totally. I remember praying and hearing His words in my mind: "I am with you, my daughter. Pray the Novena to the Sacred Heart of Jesus every day. Pray every day, and do not worry."

"Ask and it will be given to you, seek and you will find, knock and the door will be opened to you." (Matt. 7:7)

A few days later, it was time for my follow-up appointment with my surgeon. A truly kind friend took off work to drive me to the appointment, so I did not have to go alone. The surgeon took out my stitches and told me that things were healing up well. He then gave me the devastating news about my condition. He told me that they found cancer in sixteen lymph nodes, which meant that the cancer had spread to other parts of my body, and I needed chemotherapy. I asked for the prognosis, and he stated that the surgery gave me a 50 percent chance of living five years or more. He told me that was a general statistic, and every case is different. He made an appointment for a visit with an oncologist.

When I met with the oncologist, I remember that she was an Indian woman with an accent. Her manner was professional but distant. When I asked for a statistic regarding my prognosis she stated, "Hope for the best, but be prepared for the worst." She explained the chemotherapy process to me, that I would be infused every other Wednesday for six months. After the infusion on a Wednesday, I would get hooked up with a fanny back full of another round of chemo that would be pumped into my body through my port until Friday around noon. Then I would return to the office to get unhooked from the chemo bag that was empty and receive an injection in my abdomen. I was in a daze and really did not understand what was happening because I was so overwhelmed. I remember praying to God and asking for a complete recovery and for the chemo treatment to be tolerable.

"You are the God who performs miracles, you display your power among the peoples." (Psalm 77:14)

I went home and as most people these days, I googled my cancer diagnosis. I found out from reading literature on the computer that my stage was IIIC. That meant that I had about a 26 percent chance of living five years or more. I was appalled at those written words and felt helpless and lost. I remember thinking that God can perform miracles and got on my knees in my bedroom in front of my bed. I asked for a miracle healing and to live out a long and healthy life. I also bargained with God again and promised to turn my life over to Him completely if it was His will for me to be healed by His hand. After praying those words, "I will turn my life over to you," I realized that my proposal to God was an incredibly significant promise. I was willing to do whatever I could to remain on this earth for a while longer.

"He performs wonders that cannot be fathomed, miracles that cannot be counted." (Job 5:9)

"The Lord replied, "My Presence will
go with you, and I will give you rest.""
(Exod. 33:14)

I felt some comfort after prayer but still hung on to some fear because I just could not let go completely and let God take it fully. I remember that my prayers were constant, almost every minute of my waking hours. I prayed every prayer I knew and always the Novena to the Sacred Heart of Jesus and the Divine Mercy Chaplet. I listened to praise music and read scripture and uplifting messages. My sisters and family came to my house and filled it full of spiritual wall hangings, crosses, and books about God and Jesus.

I felt closer to God during this time of prayer and reflection, but I remember that I did not get still and listen for His voice. I did not allow myself to let God tell me what was on His heart for me. Regardless, I continued to pray and felt some relief just knowing He was there for me, and I felt His loving hand upon me.

My oncologist informed me that I was anemic from the cancer sucking blood from my body and expelling it in my stools. I had no idea I was anemic, but I had almost fainted several times. I was infused with iron twice on two different days. The loss of blood was something that made me feel very tired, but it was not too bad, considering what my expectations were at that time.

My oncologist sent me to another general surgeon to get my port in place. I asked if I could do it under a local numbing shot, but she said no because it was a delicate procedure. I remember feeling miffed because of the extra time it was going to take, as well as the extra expense. The procedure was scheduled for next week. When I arrived at the hospital, the entire procedure was a little over an hour.

I looked over at the top left side under my shoulder and above my left breast. I saw the port there, and it had a bandage on it. It was not uncomfortable, but you could see it sticking out from my skin. I went home, still praying for God to make this journey of cancer healing to be easy and for me to live a long and productive life. I continued to ask God for a total healing and that I would turn my life completely toward Him if that was granted to me. I guess you could say that I was in the bargaining stage of grief and promising God my life if He healed me. However, deep in my heart, I believed that He could heal me.

> "So do not fear, for I am with you; do not be dismayed, for I am your God. I will strengthen you and help you; I will uphold you with my righteous right hand." (Isa. 41:10)

I asked for prayers from my mother and her church, my sisters and their churches, and my close friends. Although my family was incredibly supportive, they lived in Austin, about four hours away. Therefore, it was just me and God in my house during my recovery period. I read scripture and started to listen for God's words. He said,

> "Fear not, for I am with you; be not dismayed, for I am your God." (Isaiah 41:10)

I felt some solace in His presence but was still unsure of my outcome.

The Treatment

It was time for my first treatment at the oncologist's office. The staff were sweet and friendly. However, the doctor was all business. I was thinking that she knew the odds were not in my favor, and she did not want to get too close to me. She told me that there was a high probability that the cancer would spread to my liver, but we would need to wait and see. I had no idea what that meant, but I made a mental note to google that for the information I needed when I got home. The nurse checked my weight, took my blood, and said that before I got infused, I had to get my blood sample analyzed.

The nurse took me into a large room with recliners and IV poles all around. There were a few people there getting their infusions all together in the room. It struck me as odd that everyone was together, and there was not much confidentiality in that setup. However, I struck up conversations with the other patients, which helped me tolerate the procedure.

The doctor had ordered nausea medication to be infused first and then steroids. I declined steroids because of the terrible way they made me feel. The nausea drip lasted about an hour to an hour and a half. After that, three pouches of chemotherapy were infused in me. The whole procedure took about six or seven hours. At the end of the infusion,

I was connected with a fanny pack that contained another pouch of chemotherapy. The pouch had a pump in it and a line that ran from the chemo bag to my port. I got infused from Wednesday morning until Friday around 3:00 PM. When they unhooked my port on Friday, I had to get an injection in my stomach to increase my white blood cells that typically decline during the chemotherapy treatment.

The first infusion was a breeze. I felt no discomfort or illness at all. I was thinking, "I got this—no big deal." However, the next appointment was totally different. As soon as the nurse hooked up my chemo to my port, I started to feel deathly ill. It was like having the flu, but worse. I had severe nausea, along with a weird sort of headache, weakness, and mental confusion that took over. I was so sick I could not even eat a saltine cracker. It was like I was in hell. I felt extremely sick from Wednesday morning until Friday at noon. I felt sick and weak during my "off" days, but I really dreaded every infusion day because I knew that I would be deathly ill. Again, I turned to God and asked Him why I had cancer and why I had to undergo chemotherapy. I remember Him telling me, "It is a trial by fire. You will come out stronger; trust in Me." I trusted Him but had no idea why He allowed me to get cancer.

> "These have come so that the proven genuineness of your faith—of greater worth than gold; which perishes even though refined by fire-may result in

> praise, glory and honor when Jesus
> Christ is revealed." (1 Pet. 1:7)

I made friends with the fellow patients in the infusion room. There was not a lot to do, and I was too sick to read. I remembered a young woman named Nancy with long brown hair, who had colon cancer like I did. She came to get infused with her mother on the same day as me. I remember thinking how sweet it was that her mother was with her. They always ate lunch together, and I was jealous that she had her mother with her and that she was able to eat lunch without getting sick.

One day she told me, "It spread to my liver."

I told her, "I'm so sorry."

She stated, "Well, I just have to deal with it." A few weeks later I noticed that she was not there anymore. I was too afraid to ask what happened, and I knew that the nurse could not tell me any way due to confidentiality. However, I said a private prayer for Nancy and asked that God take care of her soul. Then it hit me: I could be the next one to die. Oh, how I dreaded the thought.

It was not that I was unsure about where I would go. I knew that I would go to heaven. It was the thought of leaving my children behind and a nagging and persistent feeling that God had something especially important He wanted me to do. I chuckled because I thought that dying was kind of like taking a trip on an airplane. It takes a while, but when you arrive, you are at a beautiful place. I never liked traveling on planes because I got nervous about being on time and nervous about the integrity of the plane. I thought to myself, "If I'm nervous about a plane ride, a trip to heaven would be even harder." However, I stopped thinking about dying and turned to thoughts of living. I began to believe that God was going to save me, despite the poor odds modern medicine provided me.

I was working at a local school district as a school psychologist part time, thirty hours per week. I had ample sick time to get my infusions, without it costing me money for time off. I also worked part time at a pediatrician's office as a private practice psychologist. I decided to work after my infusions, to see three patients at 4:00, 5:00, and 6:00 P.M. I figured I could go home and lie around, thinking about being sick, or I could do something constructive by helping people through my counseling.

I hid the fact that I had cancer from my patients. I did not want them to think it was all about me—I was there for them. I began to lose my hair, and I purchased a wig. My head itched, and I was told by my oncologist it was because I was losing my hair. It may seem like vanity, but losing your hair is a big deal. My skin was grey and ashen, and my hair was thinning day by day. I felt sick, weak, and helpless at times. I was walking a journey I did not want to be on, but for some reason God allowed me to get cancer, and I began to trust in Him that it was not a mistake and some good would come from my situation.

"And we know that in all things God
works for the good of those who love

> him, who have been called according
> to his purpose." (Rom. 8:28)

The weeks passed, and each infusion was one less I had to go through. Friends dropped meals off for me, and my family came to visit me when they were able to do so. However, it was mainly God and me, and we got close. I went to mass every Sunday and asked for the deacon to pray for me, and he did. I did not spread the word to too many people because it was a difficult subject and a very personal journey. I read scripture and began to open my heart up to God's healing grace.

Every few weeks, I underwent a CT scan of my chest and abdomen. Every time the results were read—to the oncologist's surprise—the cancer had not spread. I was praising and thanking God for each little miracle. Then one day, I went in for an infusion, and the nurse took my blood. It was a few minutes later that my oncologist rushed into the room and said I needed to go to the hospital immediately because my platelet level was extremely low. I asked if I could go home and get my things, but she said, "No, my nurse is calling the hospital right now. Go straight to the hospital, and they will give you a transfusion." I found out that I was in danger of bleeding to death because my platelet level was so low.

When I arrived at the hospital, I was greeted by a very friendly nurse. She gave me a wonderful lunch and explained about the two pints of blood I was to receive. She said, "it's from the same donor." I have the rarest type of blood, AB+, so I was happy they had a match on hand. She hooked me up with a pouch containing the blood, and to get two pints took nearly six hours. I did not feel any differently but was able to go home that evening after the procedure was completed. I remember feeling as if I skipped school as a child. I escaped one day that I would have gotten extremely ill. However, I then realized that I still had to do the infusion; it would be added on to the end, and there was no escape. However, for a while, I got to enjoy the day without feeling ill.

Week by week passed, and my hair continued to thin out. I looked at the wig in my bathroom, wondering if I should put it on, or hide my head with scarves and hats. I chose to get my hair cut short and allowed no coloring. I wore scarves and hats. My face appeared dull and ashen, and my hair was gray (something that I had covered up since age thirty). I never used the wig, but I felt so unattractive. It was hard to face people, so I only ventured out when I had to work and when I had to go to my doctor's appointments.

I realized that my appearance was the least of my worries and that I needed to thank God for each day. When you stare death in the face, it is amazing how each day is truly a gift directly from God. I began to praise God every morning I awakened, and I was thankful for the gift of life. I started praising Him for all the good things He gave me. I was in awe of how many things just came together without my asking for them. Getting paid time off from work was a blessing, as well as meals from friends, prayers from many people, and some extra money my sister gave me for the time I took off work during my operation. I was truly blessed and started praising God and saying prayers of Thanksgiving. I started to believe that a miracle was possible and that I would live to be an old lady!

I remember that the worst feeling was not having a husband or man by my side when I was facing my cancer. I realized that it was all my fault because I did not cultivate that type of relationship. God started working on me, and I began to realize that He hit me over the head with a two by four to get my attention. Cancer was God's way of telling me to slow down, stop casually dating men, really turn to Him, and fully follow the teachings of my Catholic faith. I began to turn my life around. I remember getting great comfort from attending mass and praying and singing—and especially taking the Holy Eucharist.

> "I will praise God's name in song and glorify Him with Thanksgiving."
> (Ps. 69:30)

Finally, the day came—the day of my last infusion. I was overjoyed and completely in awe of myself for enduring such a difficult trial. I had chemo brain, which caused memory deficits, poor coordination, dizziness, spelling problems, and confusion. I also had peripheral neuropathy, which is nerve damage from the chemotherapy. My fingertips were numb, and the bottom of my feet were also numb. My chemo brain improved somewhat, but the numbness from the chemo never left my hands and feet. My doctor wanted to give me some medicine for the numbness. I took it for a few days, but it caused severe lethargy and sleepiness. Therefore, I decided to forgo the medication and deal with the symptoms, which were the result of permanent nerve damage.

My mother and three wonderful sisters took me to a quaint and rustic town in the hill country of Texas in March 2014. It was a celebration for my making it through my cancer treatment. I wore a hat to disguise my thin hair and enjoyed the shops and wildflowers of Texas and sat in a wonderful field of blue bonnets. I was praising God for no cancer found on my last CT scan.

After a few months and a several clean CT scans, the next part of my cancer treatment involved getting my port taken out. I called the surgeon's office, and the staff said they would schedule a surgery at the hospital. I complained that it would cost too much and would waste a whole day. I begged to have the surgeon take out my port with a local shot instead. The secretary put me on hold and asked the doctor. He reluctantly agreed but said that if there were any problems, he would need to do it under general anesthesia. I arrived for the appointment on time, at 9:00 a.m.

He began giving me shots around my port that numbed my tissue. He started cutting, and all I can remember is taking my mind to my "happy place" on the beach. He tugged and cut and pulled on my tissue and stated, "Well, I really put this one in deep." I stayed as still as I could because I did not want to go to the hospital. Finally, after twenty minutes of cutting and pulling, he got it out. He stitched me up, and to this day I have a very light scar that is barely noticeable. In fact, my colon surgery left me with a one-inch scar on my belly button; that was it!

Life was going back to normal slowly. I still felt sick and weak, but I kept on going, not letting my health hold me back. Work was busy and fulfilling, and I did not talk much about my cancer with anyone. I kept praying to God for a complete healing because although I had clean CT scans, I was told that the cancer could come back at any time and that I would need frequent scans to ensure my health. I decided not to rush back to dating, but to carefully choose a respectful man who was a strong Christian.

Enhancing My Spiritual Life

God began nudging me to join a prayer group. I turned to my parish, a large Catholic church in North Texas. I saw on the website that there were about four different prayer groups to call and join. I was not sure what prayer group to join, so I just started calling the numbers. I called the first three groups, but no one answered the phone. I left messages and decided that the one God wanted me to go to would respond back to me first. I was reluctant to call the last group because it was called "Charismatic Prayer Group." I felt intimidated by that name because my understanding of charismatic Christians was that they were loud and boisterous, they spoke in tongues which I thought was strange, and they were very different in the way they prayed and worshiped.

I decided to call their number because I felt that God would lead me to the right group. At my amazement, a woman answered the call after just one ring. Her name was Alice, and she was excited and happy that I called. I asked about coming to the group but said that I was not charismatic. She said to come and join the group, and the fact that I was not charismatic did not matter. She gave me the directions about where to go and the time for the prayer meeting. I felt nervous anticipation, along with some excitement and curiosity about where I was headed.

> "Then you will call on me and come
> and pray to me, and I will listen to you."
> (Jer. 29:12)

The first day I went to the charismatic prayer group on Sunday evening at the Catholic church, I walked in very cautiously. I am typically outgoing and confident, but for some reason I felt shy and a little intimidated. I did not know what to expect. To my surprise, everyone there was truly kind, and I could feel their love in the air. It was not as wild and loud as I expected, and they started out singing songs of praise to our Lord. I thought, "Well, this is pretty good, I can get into this!" Next, they started praising God with words, and I heard some people quietly speaking in tongues, but nothing overwhelming. I was given a piece of paper and a pen for the listening session. I was told that is when you are still and listen for God's words. Hmm, I wondered how to differentiate between my thoughts and God's words. I listened to everyone share what they heard from the Lord, and it was very encouraging. I did not feel ready to write anything down and share it with the group, but it gave me the message that it was important to quiet your mind and not just pray to God but to set your mind up to *listen* to God's words.

I realized that prayer is one of the ways in which we unify with God. It is the process by which we are moved by God's spirit. Without prayer, it is impossible to lead a proper spiritual life and keep up the work of the Holy Spirit. Prayer keeps us connected to God, and we should constantly praise Him because He is worthy of all praise! The more we pray, the more we will receive guidance and answers from God and lead a life that is in accordance with His will.

The next prayer group time arrived, and I happily entered the room. Everyone remembered my name, but I could not for the life of me remember anyone except Alice, the woman that answered the phone. Maybe it was because of my chemo brain. I remembered Alice's name because she said she was "Alice from Alice," and I knew that town in south Texas. We began the usual format of the group, which was to sing songs of praise to God, praise him with words, and then go into our listening session. This time, I was pre-pared to really try and see if God would give me some words through my mind if I got still and listened for His words. I praised God for saving me and for being my loving Father. I praised Jesus for dying for my sins, and I praised the Holy Spirit for giving me guidance.

> "And the people all tried to touch him,
> because power was coming from him
> and healing them all." (Luke 6:19)

I quieted my mind for a while and got the following statement in my mind,

> "He says, "Be still, and know that I
> am God; I will be exalted among the
> nations, I will be exalted in the earth."
> (Ps. 46:10).

It went over and over in my mind, and I wrote it down. I felt compelled to share it with the group and then realized that maybe there was something to this charismatic approach. I did not tell anyone in the group that I was suffering from cancer because I just did not feel comfortable about disclosing that fact. I just wanted a place to pray and worship God and to grow closer to Him. The charismatic prayer group offered that to me, and I was grateful for this group of amazing, faith-filled people! They soon became remarkably close to me, and we called each other brother and sisters in Christ. It was almost like a family of faith-filled believers!

> "Do not be anxious about anything, but
> in every situation, by prayer and peti-
> tion, with thanksgiving, present your
> requests to God. 7And the peace of God,

which transcends all understanding,
will guard your hearts and your minds
in Christ Jesus." (Phil. 4:6-7)

The Transforming Healing from Jesus through the Holy Spirit

The charismatic prayer group talked about having a Life in the Spirit Seminar. This is a seminar for people who are not charismatic to learn more about God's love, salvation from Jesus Christ, and the incredible assistance and gifts that the Holy Spirit can provide us. I learned so much more about my Heavenly Father, Jesus, and especially the Holy Spirit. The thing that helped me feel comfortable was that everything that I was taught was consistent with scripture and my Catholic faith.

I learned about the gifts of the Holy Spirit, and I felt that God wanted to give one or more to me, but I was like a baby starting to walk. I needed to have help and guidance in getting baptized in the Holy Spirit and understanding my spiritual gifts. The fifth week of the seminar was the culmination point when people pray over you to be baptized in the Holy Spirit, and you learn and understand what gifts God has bestowed upon you. I remember having dinner with my sponsor and a few others before the meeting during which we would be prayed over. The leader of the group, Leah, told me that during prayer and listening, God had told her what my gifts were, but that she could not tell me because I had to experience it myself. I felt like it was

Christmas eve, and it was nearly time to open presents. I could not wait for that time to come!

When I entered the group, we briefly met as a large group. Then, we were placed into small groups in chairs that were in a circle formation. I saw how women placed their hands and prayed over the first woman, and they also anointed her with blessed oil on her forehead and hands. I saw her begin to cry, and she began speaking in tongues. I was not intimidated at all but was ready for my turn.

My heart was beating fast, and I realized it was my turn to be prayed over. Leah and a couple of other women were there, surrounding my chair. She asked, "What do you want from Jesus?" I immediately became overwhelmed with emotion and began crying. I did not feel sad, just a feeling of intense emotion and love. I stated, "I want to be baptized in the Holy Spirit and I want to know what my spiritual gifts are." They began praying over me and speaking in tongues. I remember this strong tingling feeling coming over my body. Then, an intense heat came through every part of my body. I felt like my body was on fire, and even my ears felt like they had an iron on them. I stated, "What is this heat, I feel really hot?" This is very unusual for me because I am usually very cold and always wear a sweater. It felt like it was the Fourth of July at the equator. I cannot tell you in words how hot I felt. However, I also felt like this presence of love was inside me, and I could not stop crying because I was overwhelmed with emotion.

I began to hear the words, "My daughter, you have the gifts of wisdom and knowledge; my daughter you have the gifts of wisdom and knowledge." I stated out loud what was going around in my head to the group. Leah answered, "That's right, you do have the gifts of wisdom and knowledge; and you are cured from cancer, and it is never coming back!" *Wow,* I thought, *no one knew I had cancer, and I just got healed?* I was also overwhelmed and amazed and extremely grateful. I asked, "You knew I had cancer?" Leah responded with, "I just say what the Holy Spirit tells me, and this is truth. You are healed of your cancer, and it is not ever coming back. You also have the gifts of wisdom and knowledge."

After everyone was prayed over in my group, Leah came back to me and explained more about the gifts of wisdom and knowledge and how I could use those gifts to help others in my psychology practice. She said that I would get information about my patients from God, and there would be no way to know the information on my own. She further stated that besides the knowledge, I would be given wisdom about what to share with my patients and how to share it. Leah told me that these gifts were given to me to enhance my therapy and to tap into the healing power of Jesus in my work with my patients.

It took me a while to grow into my gifts. I began praying on a regular basis, several times per day. I also had listening sessions in which I prayed and listened for God's words that I wrote down in a journal Leah had given me. I was excited to actually hear what God wanted me to hear. I slowly learned how to discern God's words through the Holy Spirit, which is the perfect mind of God, from my own thoughts. I turned to my brothers and sisters in Christ and learned that words from the Holy Spirit are repetitive, they are consistent with scripture, and they are used to uplift the body of Christ. It was as if I learned a new avenue through which to connect with God. The Holy Spirit gave me words that were not just vague themes, but actual sentences that were given to me word by word. I used a pencil and my journal but later learned to use my computer. It was amazing how much guidance I received from the Lord. I was also developing a strong connection with every member of the prayer group.

I also received guidance from God about what was on his heart for me that day. I tried extremely hard to hold up my end of the bargain. I wanted to turn my life over to Him completely. I felt invigorated that not only could I pray, sing praises, and worship Him, but I could also learn to hear what He wanted me to know. It was so amazing, and I wanted to grow and grow into the wonderful gifts that I received from God. I also changed my personal life and stopped dating men for a while. I went to church every week and sometimes more often. I felt such peace worshiping in my church. I went to church alone and often wished I was holding hands with my beloved who was a strong Catholic man.

> "Every good and perfect gift is from above, coming down from the Father of the Heavenly lights, who does not change like shifting shadows."
> (James 1:17)

Expanding My Gifts

Later, I prayed for God to provide me with additional gifts if He so desired me to have them. I had the opportunity to pray for a friend named Rebecca who was on her deathbed in the hospital in Denver, Colorado. She had late-stage ovarian cancer and was extremely ill. She had sepsis and the cancer had spread to her liver and it was inoperable. I was friends with her brother Jim who was beside Rebecca in the hospital, and he was talking to me over the phone. I remember praying over the phone for Rebecca, and then God gave me an image in my mind of Jesus standing over her with his hand right over her heart. Jesus was waiting patiently for her to ask Him to come into her heart. Her brother was a believer and a Catholic, but she did not believe in God. However, my friend Jim told her the image that I had, and she responded with, "Really ... cool ... OK."

Rebecca did not want to have surgery because there were many blood vessels around her liver tumor, and she had a high probability of dying on the operating table. I suppose she was more open to trusting Jesus at that time. I also think that just a mustard seed of faith allowed her to be open to the healing power of Jesus Christ through the Holy Spirit. After I prayed for her over the phone and her brother continued to pray for her, she went to sleep for the night. I also had my small prayer group pray for her, too.

My friend Jim called me the next day with amazing news. He said that the doctor did a CT scan of Rebecca, and the tumor in her liver was completely gone! They had no medical explanation. Additionally, she was getting stronger despite having sepsis the day before. All in all, it was a true miracle. She walked out of the hospital four days later with no cancer at all. She also returned to her job as an electrician the next week and was climbing on buildings and doing a great job that required a lot of physical exertion.

I praised Jesus for saving Rebecca. I knew at that point that I had the gift of healing. However, I knew that I was simply a conduit or a vessel through whom Jesus Christ healed others by the Holy Spirit. I remember praying for God and Jesus to keep me humble and to give all the praise and glory to Them for the healing because it was not me; it was Them!

It was extremely exciting for me to use this gift on a daily basis with my patients. I always asked my patients if there were any cultural or spiritual issues that could impact their treatment. Many said no, but some said yes, they wanted a Christian approach combined with their counseling. When a patient agreed to a Christian approach in our counseling sessions, I used specific empirically derived protocols as a psychologist to help them get better. However, we also incorporated prayer and talked of scripture and other things consistent with the person's faith. I prayed for God to send me people who needed me, and I prayed for each patient at the beginning of the day to have steps toward healing. I prayed for every and all patients, even atheists. I prayed for atheists to receive their healing silently in my mind. I learned I am not to judge their journey or relationship with God. God loves all his children, even those who do not acknowledge him. I realized that was true because even atheists were getting healed.

I made it a regular practice to pray for my patients at the beginning of the day and before their sessions. I prayed for their healing, totally and completely. I also praised the Lord for all my blessings, and it seemed like people coming to see me were also encountering God because they were getting better from their depression, anxiety, and other types of psychological issues. I felt like Jesus was my co-therapist and my lead therapist because I often prayed silently to Him for guidance in what to say and do for each patient that I viewed as sent from God to me for a specific purpose.

> "Do not neglect the spiritual gifts you received through prophecy when the body of elders laid their hands on you." (1 Tim. 4:14)

> "To one there is given the Spirit a message of wisdom, to another a message of knowledge by the same Spirit, to another faith by the same Spirit, to another gifts of healing by that one Spirit." (1 Cor. 12:8–9)

Using My God-Given Gifts

One day a woman named Karen came to me for counseling and help at my office. She had been married for over thirty years, and despite being a dedicated wife to her husband, he divorced her. Her divorce was five years before she saw me, but she was still very hurt and broken. She had turned to drinking wine as a way of coping with her pain. She knew it was not the right thing to do, but in her isolation, it was the only thing that gave her temporary solace. She had been charged with a DWI, and she was desperate for help. She had tried other counselors but felt as though she received little help from them.

Karen was a Christian woman with a deep faith, but she was off track a bit. She was in severe emotional pain, and I knew it was difficult for her to come in and see me and admit to all the problems she had been experiencing. I praised her for coming in and being brave. I listened to her story and saw the intense pain in her face, and through her tears, I knew she was lonely and felt abandoned and unloved. I gave her comfort but felt that at that very moment what she needed was to experience God's love. I showed her a short video of scripture that focused on our heavenly Father's love for us, that she is His child, and that He wants to lavish His love on her, simply because she is His child, His creation. Her life is not a mistake, for God made her in His image.

> "See what great love the Father has lavished on us, that we should be called children of God! And that is what we are! The reason the world does not know us is that it did not know him." (1 John 3:1)

After watching the video and talking about God's love for her, I saw a glimmer of hope in her eyes. Instead of talking to her, I asked her if I could pray for her. She immediately said, "Yes," and I held her hands and prayed for her comfort, for her to feel God's love, and to be completely and totally healed emotionally, physically, and spiritually. I knew that it was going to take a while, but I had complete faith that Jesus would heal her emotional wounds.

I was not sure if she would come back, but she came back and attended her sessions regularly with me. She began to open to healing, but it took her a while to back off from her alcohol use. Karen had an attorney and knew that eventually her case would be heard by the judge. She had no idea how long that would take, and she was advised that it could be up to a year or longer before her case was heard. Karen's motive for counseling was not to look good in front of the judge, although she knew that would help her case. She was earnestly seeking an emotional healing, and we talked and prayed together every session. For a while I had her text me yes or no if she drank. That worked somewhat, but then she decided to take the responsibility back on her own shoulders.

We talked about her work, her life, her trials, and ways to cope in a healthy way. Sometimes she would come in feeling great, at other sessions she was struggling. However, she was getting better each day, and I knew that Jesus was in the process of healing her. He was guiding my work with her, and it was because of Jesus that she reported feeling better. We both know for certain that God sent her to me, that it was not a mistake.

Karen is an amazing woman who helps the poor by making them blankets, making food for them, and giving them money. These people are living on a fixed income, and they are residents in the same apartment complex her parents live in. She is open to helping anyone that needs it. She has such an amazing heart that is so giving and wonderful.

She spoke with me about some intense anger she had toward a particular woman. She went on and on about her anger. I told her to pray for her enemy, just as Christ told us to do.

> "But I tell you, love your enemies and
> pray for those who persecute you,"
> (Matt. 5:44)

When she returned to see me at the next session, she told me that her anger went from intense anger to a low boil. Indeed, the Lord's words were true.

Karen is doing much better now. Yes, she continues her healing journey. Will she be completely healed of her depression and alcoholism? Yes, indeed! I have no doubt that Jesus will heal her completely. All praise and glory goes to Him, the perfect physician! Karen is a testament to the healing power of psychological counseling combined with prayer and a Christian approach to healing psychological issues. I pray for her before every session, and the Holy

Spirit guides my words and prayers for her every time we are together. I am thankful that God sent her to me.

Often, when I see evidence of Jesus healing people through me, and I am amazed that He has allowed me, a humble servant, just a regular person, to be part of His wonderful plan of healing people when they seek it from Him. All praise and glory to our Lord and healer Jesus Christ!

> "Jesus went through all the towns and villages, teaching in their synagogues, proclaiming the good news of the kingdom and healing every disease and sickness." (Matt. 9:35)

Turning My Life Over to God

I continued to participate in our prayer group and attend mass. I remember it was an ordinary Sunday, and I attended the 10:00 a.m. mass. When I went up for Holy Communion, a strong force pushed me down, and I fell backwards. I got back up and took the Holy Eucharist and the Precious Blood of Christ. I then heard very strongly in my mind, "You are going to be a leader of people, and you will be rebuked and reviled for what you do for Me." I distinctly heard those words and there was no doubt in my mind it was Jesus and the Holy Spirit. I went back to my seat and kneeled while praying.

I said in my mind, "Wait a minute, Jesus, did you dial the wrong number? I am shy and not a leader and what do you mean about being rebuked and reviled for what I am going to do? Just what do you want me to do?"

I was immediately given a vision of Jesus chuckling and saying, "Oh my child, you are so impatient! You will be given the knowledge and guidance to do what you need to do for me when the time is right." I felt some relief from that response, but also knew that God had some plans for me. Then I remembered my promise to God.

"God, if you save me, I will turn my life over to you completely." I was about two years post-diagnosis of cancer, and it was time to put my promise into action.

Why Does God Allow Suffering? – Working with Those Who Have Trauma

As a psychologist in private practice, I have an opportunity to treat a variety of people that come to me with various issues. I pray for God to send who ever He feels needs to see me. Therefore, I believe that everyone is sent to me for a reason and I need to do everything in my power to help them feel healed and happier, to overcome their negative symptoms and to reach their full potential. It seemed as though God was sending me many women who had experienced trauma. Trauma from childhood sexual abuse, abortion, physical abuse as a child or as an adult from domestic violence. There were many sad stories of very intense and terrible pain these women had endured. It seemed that each one of them wanted desperately to believe that God existed and that He was there for them, but many felt angry and abandoned by God. They were angry because they had reached out to Him in prayer and He did not stop the abuse.

The counseling sessions became a journey that I realized needed to involve not only a psychological healing but also a spiritual healing. It was my job, guided by the God, the Holy Spirit and Jesus Christ to weave psychological methods together with a spiritual approach.

I remember a woman that I worked with drew a picture of how she felt about the horrific sexual abuse she suffered as a child of 4 until age 12. She drew a picture of herself as a small child with her arms reaching up as if she were requesting help or to be held and comforted. Jesus was depicted in her picture as a large person who had his back facing her. She explained that she felt that Jesus turned his back to her because when she prayed and cried out to Him to end the abuse, it never stopped happening. She began to feel as if He didn't exist, or if He did exist, He didn't care about her.

It was an intense and difficult journey for myself and these abused women to traverse. I was able to help them only with the help of Jesus as my "co-therapist." I helped them realize that Jesus was always by their side, even when they were being abused. Suffering is a consequence of evil that exists in our world. Although it hurts God to see innocent people suffer, He does not bring it upon them as a punishment for wrong doing, or because He just allows suffering to happen without caring. I realized that God allows suffering because he gives us all free will, and that many times good can come out from suffering. Many times, it takes years before the good comes out, but it can take many forms. Learning to forgive and trust God again is a huge spiritual lesson. Learning to forgive others is a major spiritual lesson that Christ taught us and is appropriate for victims to apply. There is even psychological research that supports the efficacy of forgiveness therapy.

It takes a while for those who have been traumatized to work through their feelings of anger, hurt and pain. However; when the healing journey includes Jesus, it is more complete. Often these women come out closer to God than they were before the counseling. Some of the women became counselors themselves, or used their experiences to help other victims. Even though God does not answer our prayers immediately in the way we desire does not mean he is not with us and is not listening. He is with us each and every step and his love for us is immense. On the day of judgment, the perpetrators of abuse will have to face their sin. However; that is between them and God.

The women with trauma with whom I worked learned ways to get their hurt and anger out, deal with it, and not let it affect their lives in negative ways any more. Often, they learned to forgive God, trust Him again, and get closer to Him than ever before. Our God has a vision that can see what was and is and is to come. His vantage point allows the ability to see the good that can come from suffering, and that it is His will for all of his children, even those with trauma to be healed emotionally, spiritually and physically. Therefore, I choose to trust God when he brings me women broken from trauma. I trust always that their pathway to healing will be led with the light that Jesus shines on evil so it can be revealed, delt with and healed. I know that God has special blessings and graces that are bestowed upon victims of trauma.

"Chance" Encounter

O ne day I was walking from my car to the grocery store. I saw a dirty homeless man sitting in the corner right beside the store. The Lord spoke to me and said, "Go and pray for him." I argued a bit with God and said, "But he's so dirty, and he could be dangerous." I went about the store with my shopping and God would not let it go. Finally, I said, "Fine, God, I will pray for him if he is still there when I take my groceries to the car." I took my time to load my car with the groceries from my cart. I guess you could say I sort of wished he would move on and I would be off the hook. God does not work that way, and He had a job for me. I needed to be obedient to His request.

I approached the man and said, "My name is Christina, and I know you don't know me, but I was wondering: "Do you want me to pray for you?" He immediately said yes and grabbed my hand. He told me his sad story and how he was hit by a car. He had no home because he lost his job, and he was all alone. I noticed that he had a beer can in a brown bag that he was sipping. There was no judgment on my part, but I prayed over this man for him to be blessed and brought out of his poor situation. I spent about an hour with him, talking and praying. He seemed so hungry for human touch, and he told me he wanted to go to church again. I never saw this man again, so I do not know what happened, but I feel happy that I obeyed God's request for me to pray for him.

We need to always be ready to listen to God's nudges or direct requests of us. He will put us in situations where we can be used for His glory and to help others. I was going to a grocery store, and I never expected for God to call on me. After this incident, I knew that our God is an all-powerful, all knowing, and loving presence that is delighted when we answer His call to do whatever He has in mind for us at the time. Our works, large or small, can bless others beyond our comprehension. It is amazing how our God works and it is so humbling to be part of his plan when he calls out to me. I went to a grocery store and this encounter occurred! It is important to always be open to God when He calls out to us to respond to his will. It can happen anywhere at any time. Nothing is by chance, is my belief. God orchestrates situations or circumstances for us, but we use our free will to respond the way he desires us to respond, or to ignore the inner tugging of his desire for us.

> "He replied, "Blessed rather are those
> who hear the word of God and obey it."
> (Luke 11:28)

"I am the vine; you are the branches. If you remain in me and I in you, you will bear much fruit; apart from me you can do nothing." (John 15:5)

I started praying for people right and left. Sometimes they were strangers; sometimes they were not. I also volunteered at a homeless shelter and fed the homeless. I donated more money to charity. I got to speak on Catholic radio three times, and I was turning to God for every major decision.

It is not always easy, but I try very hard to put God first in my life. He has saved me for a reason. It is because of Him that I live. I got off the beaten pathway after my divorce and did not think much about God, just getting a date to help lift my spirits. I learned that true healing and love comes from God, not from random dates. I began to live my life both professionally and personally putting God first. However, I am a sinner, and it is by the blood of Christ that I am forgiven and reconciled with God. Our God is a perfect Father, and Jesus Christ is the King of mercy. I began knowing the Holy Spirit in a more intimate way as I continued to listen to the voice of God through the Holy Spirit on a regular basis.

I had been divorced and alone for ten years. After my cancer, my dating slowed down. I tried to date a couple of Catholic men, but it did not work out. However, I knew for certain that if I were to get into a serious relationship with someone, that they would need to be a Christian. I was very blessed when God sent me a truly faith-filled Catholic man who enjoyed exercising, eating healthy, and having lively discussions. Love blossomed, and I am so happy and grateful that God sent me my one true love. I am forever grateful that in this stage of my life, I have a man who really loves me, has taken the time to know me, and has helped my faith grow in leaps and bounds.

Jaime is my one true love because he loves me like Christ does. He is a wonderful man who I married in the Catholic church the day after Christmas, 2020. God is at the top of our relationship, and we have a sacramental marriage in the Catholic Church! That means that I must put my own needs aside and think about my partner's needs always. We turn to God during difficult times, and He leads us to peace and resolution of any conflicts. We also attend mass every week together, and I am so happy and proud to hold his hand when we walk into church. His faith is strong and solid, and he knows me more than any man I have ever met.

Marriage is a vocation and not for everyone. However, I prayed many nights while looking up at the moon, asking for such a man. It is not like the movies portray: "They lived happily ever after." Yes, we are happy, but it is a dynamic and ever-moving process. Learning to let go and trust him and God is a lesson for me every day. He also helps me grow spiritually, and that is one of the purposes of your spouse, to ensure you go to heaven. I am working on myself, becoming less self-centered. My husband is an engineer, and his brain works differently than mine. However, my creative, intuitive, and emotional attributes are nicely balanced with his strengths. He often brings me back to earth when my mind thinks of all sorts of possible projects or endeavors. I love my husband so very much; he is my gift from God, and I will cherish him as God's gift forever and a day! I will also take care of him like a chest of precious jewels, never to let them gather dust.

I am so excited and happy that God gave me so much through this wonderful man. He is such a great man and such a gift from God. My life is so blessed, and I am in awe of the gift of love to me. Do not get me wrong; there have been times where Jaime has created situations where I have had to look in the mirror at my own sins. I have done that and have recognized and put into practice what it means to be in a loving relationship: God first, then your partner. It is such an amazing experience at this stage of my life to have such a fantastic partner and that we are a perfect fit for each other!

During our marriage preparation, we were assigned a couple who counseled us in getting ready for marriage. We went to a Pre-Cana meeting that explained exactly what a sacramental marriage means. It is a vocation, and God intends men and women to unite with together with God at the top of your relationship. You are to love your spouse as Christ loves you and the church. It is beautiful to fully understand the meaning of a sacramental marriage. It has taught me to be less selfish, listen better, be less defensive, and give love to my beloved, using his love languages without sex. Marriage is until death do us part. Jaime has truly helped me grow in my faith, and I want to do the same thing for him.

"Out of his fullness we have all received
grace in place of grace already given."
(John 1:16)

God saved me for a reason, and every day that I live, I understand what He wants me to do that day. I am six and a half years post-surgery, which puts me in official remission! I pray that God will send me whoever needs to see me in my psychology practice. I pray for my sisters in Christ, whoever needs prayer. I pray for my staff at work, our country, and our world.

I just take it one day at a time and try my best to put God first because He performed a miracle on me and others that I have witnessed. More importantly, He loves me, and I am His child. I would not be here without Him. I was destined to die on this earth at an early age, but He allowed me to live longer on earth, and I will fulfill His desires and requests of me until the day He takes me home to our true home in heaven. I feel thankful and privileged that God is using me every day, and I will never, ever stop loving and praising Him. I am thankful for my cancer because I was refined by the fire. This was a blessing in disguise. I would never be this close to Him had it not been for my cancer diagnosis. As I have come to know, God can take a terrible situation and turn it into good. Praises to Him forever! I cannot wait to find out each day what He has in mind for me and what is on His heart. It is by the grace of God I live, and I live life to the fullest with Him at the helm of my life.

"For you God, tested us; you refined us like silver. You brought us into prison and laid burdens on our backs. You led people ride over our heads; we went through fire and water, but you brought us to a place of abundance." (Ps. 66:10-12)

"Do not be conformed to this world, but be transformed by the renewal of your mind, that by testing you may discern what is the will of God, what is good, and acceptable and perfect." (Rom.12:2)

"For since the creation of the world God's invisible qualities—his eternal power and divine nature—have been clearly seen, being understood from what has been made, so that people are without excuse." (Rom. 1:20)

The Accident

The Emergency

I t was a warm day in May 2018, and my daughter and her boyfriend had come to my psychology office to put some furniture together for me, as I had just moved into a new office. They were both on their bicycles, and my daughter was new to the sport but relished it very much. She enjoyed biking with her new beau, and he was showing her the ropes of the sport. It was close to sundown, and I encouraged them to leave and start the ride home. They finally left my office, and I stayed to complete some paperwork.

Approximately forty-five minutes after they left, I received a horrific phone call—the phone call no mother wants to hear. It was Luke, her boyfriend, on the line, and he was frantically crying. "Jessica had an accident on the bike ... It is really bad ... it's bad. I'm not sure she's breathing." I was shocked to hear those words in Luke's cracking voice. He could barely speak, and his sobbing dominated our exchange over the phone. In the background, I could hear the siren of the ambulance, and he told me they were on a back road, far away from town.

I knew exactly where they were. Their car was parked at the end of the hill, and during the final descent to their car, Jessica had gone too fast and lost her footing. She had catapulted over the top of her bike, slamming face-down on the concrete, sliding and bumping over and over until she reached the bottom of the hill. Luke told me that when he had placed his hand on her left eye and forehead to try and stop the bleeding, her entire eyebrow and a huge amount of tissue had fallen off her face. He also said that she was gagging from blood in her throat when he turned her over.

I asked Luke what hospital the ambulance was going to, and he said, "Medical City in [a nearby town]." I dropped everything I was doing and ran out of my office as fast as lightning. On the way to the hospital, I called her father, my ex-husband, and let him know what had happened. He had been in town on business and was now at the airport. He said he would make his way to the hospital.

When I arrived at the hospital, I ran into the paramedics who had brought my daughter into the emergency room. They were young-looking but very professional. I told them I was a neuropsychologist, and I understood medical details and the state of a person's brain post-injury. I held my tears back as I spoke because I wanted to hear every word they uttered, trying to remember Paul's words:

> "I can do all this through him who gives me strength." (Phil. 4:13)

They stated, "She was unresponsive to sound, pain, or touch upon arrival at the scene. She did not respond to commands and was nonverbal. She was not breathing and had shown no signs of life. We gave her an IV, and when we intubated her, she became combative."

Their report let me know that she was dead when they found her, but they were able to revive her. However, she was not expected to make it through the night, and even if she did, the chances were high that she would be severely brain damaged. She might be in a vegetative state. In that state, there are no meaningful responses or voluntary activities. Her medical condition upon arrival at the hospital showed she had a high probability of being in a vegetative state with severe damage because of the prolonged state of unresponsiveness and a lack of higher mental functions. The alternative to dying was that she would be severely disabled with permanent need for help with daily living. I also knew that most people in her condition die within twenty-four hours. A still voice whispered to me:

> "The LORD sustains them on their sickbed and restores them from their bed of illness." (Ps. 41:3)

I asked if I could see her, but the nurse immediately told me no because the trauma team was working on her to try and save her life. I was told I could wait in the waiting room or the chapel. I felt so helpless and very emotional about what was happening. I turned to my faith and placed my trust in Jesus, but it was extremely difficult not to worry. The hospital was also very stark, cold, and dreary. There was not much on the walls, the air conditioner blew out cold air, and the medical team was distant and not informative. Again scripture came to me:

> "Be anxious for nothing, but in every-thing by prayer and supplication with thanksgiving let your requests be made known to God. And the peace of God, which surpasses all comprehen-sion, will guard your hearts and your minds in Christ Jesus." (Phil. 4:6–7)

I was shocked by the information about Jessica's medical state, but I immediately turned to her boyfriend Luke who was sobbing. I knew he was an atheist but that did not stop me. I grabbed him by the hand and stated very firmly, "We are going into the chapel right now, and we are going to get on our knees and beg God to save her life!" I said it with a strong conviction and power that I knew came from the Lord. We entered the chapel that was empty. There was an altar of sorts in the room, and we kneeled before it. We were both crying, but I managed to say with strength, "Dear God in Jesus's name, please save my daughter from death. I know You are the greatest physician Jesus, and You can save her. I am asking for divine intervention and that You save her from death and give her a great outcome."

> "Then he said to her, 'Daughter, your
> faith has healed you. Go in peace.'"
> (Luke 8:48)

Luke began to pray, too. "Please God, please God, save her—she is too good to die. Please save her, God, I beg you." We prayed and prayed until a nurse entered the chapel. She said that Jessica was still in a precarious state, but that she was going to get a CT scan. I asked if I could see her, that I wanted to put my hands on her and pray, but the nurse still said no. "They are trying to save her life; you can't see her yet."

> "Heal me, LORD, and I will be healed;
> save me and I will be saved, for you are
> the one I praise." (Jer. 17:14)

> "Jesus went throughout Galilee,
> teaching in their synagogues, pro-
> claiming the good news of the kingdom,
> and healing every disease and sick-
> ness among the people. 24News about
> him spread all over Syria, and people
> brought to him all who were ill with var-
> ious diseases, those suffering severe
> pain, the demon-possessed, those
> having seizures, and the paralyzed; and
> he healed them." (Matt. 4:23-24)

I prayed some more and knew I needed support. I called my sister in Christ from my prayer group, Leah Bickel, and her husband Nick. Even though it was close to 10:00 p.m., they said that they would come right over to the hospital to pray with us for Jessica. They arrived in about thirty minutes and immediately started praying with us. The time went by quickly, but we were in constant prayer. I felt comfort from their presence and felt a glimmer of hope.

Finally, a nurse came into the chapel and stated that they received the results of the CT scan and that they could find no bleeding on her brain at that time. I felt a strong sense of relief but also disbelief, considering her condition at arrival to the hospital. Finally, the medical team let us into her room in the ER. I remember looking at her lifeless body. She had a large white endotracheal tube in her throat, and she was on a respirator. She had a white large collar around her neck. Her left eye was completely swollen shut, and there was blood coming out from her ear, eyes, and nose. She was totally unresponsive. Her face was completely covered in open wounds with no intact skin that was visible at all except around her lips. Jessica only had a small bit of her left eyebrow, and there was a large amount of tissue damage on her face, arms, and legs. When I entered the room, the surgeon was still stitching her legs up.

I had my blessed oil and wanted to anoint her forehead, but there was no visible tissue that was not damaged. Leah said just put the oil on her hairline. So, I blessed her on her head and both of her hands. Leah, Nick, Luke, and I all put our hands on her body. We all prayed to God and asked for a complete and total healing of her body and mind in the name of Jesus Christ, that she would have a perfect outcome with all her skills, and that her brain would restored to the condition it was before the accident. She was in graduate school studying psychology, and I wanted her to be able to return to college to finish her degree and work in the field. Due to her condition, I had some doubts, but I turned to Jesus in desperation and faith that He would heal her completely.

> "Jesus went through all the towns and villages, teaching in their synagogues, proclaiming the good news of the kingdom and healing every disease and sickness." (Matt. 9:35)

I remember looking over and saw the bicycle clothing that she had just proudly purchased. I pointed it out to Luke. The nurses had cut it up to tend to her wounds quickly. I looked at Luke and said, "She's going to be really mad when she finds out about this." It made me briefly chuckle and gave me a sense of relief because if she recovered to the point of realizing what happened to her bicycle outfit, she would be well enough to live a decent life.

Shortly after our prayers, they took us back to the chapel. They said that they needed to do more tests. Out of the blue, Leah stated, "She's going to be alright. It's going to take a long time for her to recover, but she is going to be fine."

I asked her, "How do you know that are you sure?"

Leah stated that she listened to the Holy Spirit, and those were the words she was given. I knew Leah for a while, and I believed without a shadow of a doubt that she heard the voice of God. Her words gave me great comfort. I praised the Lord for those words of encouragement and thanked Him for giving her a good outcome. At that time, I knew for sure that she was not going to die. I knew that I needed to continue to pray for her, but also, I needed quiet my mind to listen to God's voice. I was in a state of shock and was unable to quiet my mind in the hospital. I just continued to pray and pray for a good outcome and for her to come out of the coma.

The medical staff moved her to the ICU in the hospital. I had called my family from Austin, and my sister and mother arrived. Jessica's father and two brothers were at the hospital the next morning. My sister got Jessica a cute teddy bear with a balloon. Her father said she would be all right, that I did not need to worry. I felt as though he was in denial and did not understand how serious her injuries were. Nonetheless, I shook my head but also reminded him that she was in a coma. Jessica's boyfriend Luke never left her side. He stayed with her constantly and only left briefly to eat or use the restroom.

I never left Jessica's side, sleeping in a chair next to her bed. The next day, Jessica opened her eyes briefly. The physician said he wanted to take her off the respirator. I was so encouraged about those small steps and thanked the Lord profusely for His intervention. The physician came into the room to make his rounds and said, "This is certainly an unexpected outcome. I suppose it's because she is young, healthy, and in good shape." I felt that the doctor misunderstood the power of prayer.

I told the doctor while pointing to my cross around my neck, "You think she was lucky; I say it's because of this." He shrugged his shoulders, completed his examination, and left the room. However, the medical staff were talking among themselves in disbelief that she lived through the night and was actually improving in ways that were totally unexpected. I heard her called "young and strong," and "lucky." No one mentioned God or a miracle, yet I knew that I had witnessed one. However, I still was uneasy because her life was not yet out of the woods.

> "Then your light will break forth like the dawn, and your healing will quickly appear; then your righteousness will go before you, and the glory of the LORD will be your rear guard." (Isa. 58:8)

My mother and sister supported me greatly, but my oldest son and ex-husband left that day because they felt she was going to be fine. I prayed for a great outcome, but in my heart, I knew that we had a huge road ahead of us, and that healing from her severe injuries was not going to be easy. A few days passed, and Jessica began getting better and better. She did not have health insurance at the time of her accident, so the hospital wanted her discharged as soon as possible. She started speaking a few words, but usually she was asleep. She did not eat any food but had an IV for fluids. Eventually, she improved enough to be moved from ICU to a regular room. Again, the staff was scratching their heads and could not believe in the transformation from the severely impaired state she was in just a few days before to her current state.

Jessica was not eating or drinking much at all. When the nurse came into to check on her, she asked, "Where are you?" Jessica responded with, "Church, I think." Jessica obviously heard our prayers, and her mental state was still precarious and confused. Despite her situation and her lack of mental orientation, the hospital discharged her four days after her accident. She was taken out in a wheelchair with very minimal aftercare instructions. She clung to her teddy bear like a helpless child, and my heart ached for her because her entire body was full of scabs, and all the bones in her face were broken.

> "For I know the plans that I have for you," declares the LORD, plans for welfare and not for calamity to give you a future and a hope." (Jer. 29:11)

Her aftercare included getting her stitches out of her legs seven days later and getting the broken bones in her face checked by a physician in two weeks. She had broken nearly every bone in her face, which made eating and drinking exceedingly difficult. There was no talk of rehabilitation or an appointment with a neurologist. Luke and I were not very clear on how to care for her because she was not eating much, her vocalizations were very mixed up, and she seemed weak and vulnerable. She clung to that teddy bear that her aunt gave her with great conviction. I remember thinking of her like a little two-year-old child. That is how she appeared to me—unable to talk clearly, needing constant reassurance, and clinging to that teddy bear for emotional support.

I remembered back to Mother's Day, 2018. It was the day before her accident. She asked me what I wanted for Mother's Day. I said, "I just want you to come to church with me." She had been raised in the Catholic faith but stopped going to church on a regular basis some time before that. I recall her looking at me throughout the mass and commenting, "They changed the prayers." I felt an intense love from our heavenly Father come upon us and the presence of the Holy Spirit. We sat in the very front row, as that was my usual place of worship at the local Catholic church near our home. I introduced her to Deacon Larry with whom I felt close. He had prayed over me when I had cancer, and he was always ready to listen to me whenever I had a need. He was happy to meet Jessica, and I was so proud that she was at my side.

> "Do not withhold your mercy from me, Lord; may your love and faithfulness always protect me." (Ps. 40:11)

"But in your great mercy you did not put
an end to them or abandon them, for
you are a gracious and merciful God."
(Neh. 9:31)

We arrived home from the hospital and set her up in her bedroom. We had water in a cup with a straw and medicine to put on her sores. She spent approximately eighteen to twenty hours asleep each day. I knew that it was typical for people with traumatic brain injuries to sleep a lot, but I thought that was excessive. I called our family physician and was told it was to be expected. Luke and I had to wake her up to sip water. She did so very reluctantly, and she had to be encouraged because any movement that involved her face caused her great pain. Some pain pills had been prescribed for her, but they made her even more groggy and disoriented. However, we gave them to her because we did not want to see her suffer.

"Even though I walk through the darkest valley, I will fear no evil, for you are with me; your rod and your staff, they comfort me." (Ps. 23:4)

Meeting in Heaven

One evening when I was about to pray over Jessica, she stated to me with an innocent voice, "Mom, I was kicked out of heaven." Luke was there, and he listened intently. I asked her what she meant, and she said, "I was standing beside the gate to heaven, and they said I couldn't come in yet because it wasn't my time." They said I had to go back, but I really wanted to stay there; it felt so nice." I asked her for more details because that really sparked my interest. However, she said she did not want to talk about it anymore because she was tired. I anointed her with blessed oil, said my prayers over her, tucked her in, and she went to bed. She never mentioned it again, but it seemed so real at the time that I believed that she was speaking the truth.

> "When Jesus had said these things, He cried out with a loud voice, 'Lazarus, come forth.' The man who had died came forth, bound hand and foot with wrappings, and his face was wrapped around with a cloth. Jesus said to them, "Unbind him, and let him go." (John 11:43-44)

> "Now the crowd that was with him when he called Lazarus from the tomb and raised him from the dead continued to spread the word. Many people,

because they had heard that he had
performed this sign, went out to meet
him." (John 12:17–18)

The Sunday after her accident, I went to mass alone at Immaculate Conception Church. I met Deacon Larry after mass in the narthex. I told him about the accident that Jessica had experienced the past Monday after Mother's Day. He became still and quiet, but tearful, and then he told me something remarkable.

He stated, "I saw your daughter at mass last Sunday. She kept looking at you and could not keep her eyes from looking at you. It was then that I saw the Holy Spirit descend upon you and your daughter.

I said, "Really?" It was so hard to believe, but I knew his integrity and faith, and I knew he was speaking the truth. It made me think that due to that experience, the Holy Spirit was with us both, and that was why she took a trip to heaven but was sent back. I tried to get Jessica to tell me more, but she was not open to discussing this further, so I let it drop. However, I knew in my heart that what she spoke was truth, and I was so happy.

The Healing Journey

Luke canceled all his classes for the summer and the following fall. His job was to take care of Jessica full time until she was completely recovered. I had to return to work to make money to pay the bills, but I was with her as much as possible. Luke had to guide her to use the restroom and assist her with that process. He had to wake her up to eat soft foods like yogurt and mashed potatoes. I recall feeding her one evening, and it was like she was a baby. She refused to take in the full amount of yogurt on the spoon and let it fall out of her mouth. I begged her to eat but was only able to get her to eat a few bites of food. She was losing weight and was nearly skin and bones due to her lack of eating.

At that time, I prayed over her daily, at least three times a day. I prayed for her constantly during the day when I was at work. I thanked God for allowing Luke to be her full-time caretaker. If he had not done that, I would have had to hire a nurse to care for her. Luke was showing her unconditional love. Even though he was not a professed Christian, his love and dedication to my daughter reminded me of the love of Christ. I was so impressed and in awe of his unselfish dedication to her healing. He was always at her side, and his full-time job was to take perfect care of her every minute of the day and night. I also remembered his prayers to God to save her life and hoped secretly that he would be converted to a believer.

I contacted my previous supervisor, a clinical neuropsychologist who supervised me during my internship and post-doc fellowship, telling him what happened, and he graciously allowed one of his colleagues to give her a neuropsychological evaluation about one-month post-accident. The results were devastating but not surprising. She had severe neurocognitive impairment with depression and behavioral disturbance. Her memory, attention span, executive functions, and processing speed were severely impaired, and all other functions were impaired to some degree. It was strongly recommended that she not return to graduate school. She had just finished her first year, working on her master's degree in counseling psychology.

Her professors at the university were truly kind and understanding. They allowed her to recover over the summer and work on her thesis. Two of her professors came to our home to meet with us. They said they would accommodate her in any way and that she had up to six years to finish her degree. It was decided that she would work on her thesis, and then see how she was in the fall. Their support and concern were very touching.

Jessica was getting stronger and stronger each day. My mother came to stay with us for about three weeks. She wrote down in a log everything that happened every day. There were small victories every day, such as talking to us in a way that made sense, walking to the bathroom alone, eating more, and drinking fluids. Right after the accident she was very sleepy, and it was almost like force feeding her soft foods, such as yogurt, mashed potatoes, and her favorite dish, split pea soup. It reminded of me when she was a baby; I would place a small bit of food on a spoon, and she would only take a small portion of the food on the spoon. Luke and I encouraged her each day, but because several bones in her face were broken, it was very painful for her to eat and to drink from a straw. She was unable to drink from a glass until much later in her healing. She maintained the voice of a child, incredibly soft spoken and fragile, and she appeared so innocent. My heart went out to her, and I wished I could carry her pain. However, I prayed over her several times a day, stroked her hair, and gave her a lot of TLC to help her feel better.

Morning glories in Christianity represent rebirth.

"For God so loved the world that he gave his one and only Son, that whoever believes in him shall not perish but have eternal life." (John 3:16)

One evening when I was praying over her, she said, "Mom, I don't have an eyebrow. I want my eyebrow back."

I asked her, "Sweetie, do you want us to ask God for your eyebrow?"

She replied, "Yes," so we prayed that God would restore her face to the way it was before her accident. She seemed happy with that intervention, and soon after that prayer was recited several times, her eyebrow began to grow back over the scar that was left on her forehead. Her scars on her face slowly disappeared, and her face was turning back to the way it was before the accident, despite the deep wounds she had sustained from the accident.

> "Is anyone among you sick? Then he must call for the elders of the church and they are to pray over him, anointing him with oil in the name of the Lord." (James 5:14)

My mom left to go back to Austin, and Luke kept me up to date on everything that was happening with Jessica's recovery. I was forced to go back to work to bring money in for our living expenses. Luke and I took Jessica to get her stitches out at our family physician's office, but the scab had grown over the stitches. It made the removal exceedingly difficult, but her kind physician assistant was able to remove them without much pain. He also suggested that she consider cognitive rehabilitation. We also followed up with the facial specialist, and this physician stated that no intervention was needed because her bones were healing fine.

> "Let us then approach God's throne of
> grace with confidence, so that we may
> receive mercy and find grace to help us
> in our time of need." (Heb. 4:16)

I went to my charismatic prayer group and asked for prayers for my Jessica. Everyone said a prayer for her that night and agreed to pray for her on a regular basis until she was healed. All of us at the prayer group believed in the healing power of Jesus Christ through the Holy Spirit. We all expected and believed that a total and complete healing was possible. Several people came up to me over the weeks and months of her recovery and stated, "She is going to be OK. Her recovery will take a long time, but she will be fine."

It was very reassuring to understand that she was going to be fine. I really believed everyone at my prayer group, and their prayers were appreciated so much because I believed with great conviction the power that each prayer had to change things. I had a total of three different people approach me from my prayer group and tell me that the Lord spoke to them and asked whether they could pray over Jessica. I arranged for the each to come at an individual time, and she allowed them to pray over her. It was amazing because each person individually said that the Holy Spirit spoke to them and told them she would be completely healed, but it would take a while.

> "At sunset, the people brought to Jesus
> all who had various kinds of sickness,
> and laying his hands on each one, he
> healed them." (Luke 4:40)

A few weeks later, I had a Bible study at my home. There were approximately seven women who came to my house to discuss 1 Corinthians. It was a beautiful group full of faith-filled women. The subject came up about Jessica, and they all asked if we could pray for her. I asked her, and she seemed a little shy about it, but she allowed everyone to place their hands on her and pray for her total healing. In my mind, every prayer counted, and I welcomed everyone's willingness to ask God for her healing. I felt power in the numbers and felt the Holy Spirit moving over us in a big way.

Sometimes a mother knows something without words. I guess it is the mother's intuition that God gives us. At that point after the prayer, I let go of my doubts and totally embraced the idea that Jessica was going to recover completely. However, I was not naive, and I knew that a great deal of time and effort was to be exerted before she would be declared healed. She had already broken out of the mold of her grim prognosis, and I was thrilled with how well she was doing thus far.

One evening when I was at a prayer group meeting at my parish, we got into small groups to pray. I remember Hector was our leader of the four people in our group. He asked if anyone needed prayer. I volunteered immediately and said that my daughter Jessica needed prayers. We all held hands, and Hector prayed out loud for Jesus to restore her health so that she would be as she was before the accident. I felt an immediate heat and tingling that I often feel from the Holy Spirit when it comes upon me. I felt that heat, and I welcomed that heat because to me, it was a visible sign that that the Holy Spirit was with us. After the prayer, I felt peace, and Hector stated again what I had been told: "You daughter will be totally healed, but it will take a while."

This was music to my ears, and I remembered driving home from the meeting listening to praise music on my radio. This verse came to mind:

> "Hear this, you kings! Listen you rulers!
> I, even I, will sing to the LORD; the God
> of Israel, in song." (Judg. 5:3)

"I will both lie down in peace, and sleep;
For You alone, O Lord, make me dwell
in safety." (Ps. 4:8)

Jessica was not progressing in her cognitive healing as fast as she desired. She often had memory lapses, word-finding problems, and frustration. At times, she would explode in anger, which later turned to tears and then remorse. I knew her behavior was directly linked to her brain injury, but it was still difficult for us all. I prayed for a healing but also made an appointment with a rehabilitation neurologist from UT Southwestern Medical School. She finally got an appointment, and we were excited to have such a prestigious clinic provide care for my daughter. Her boyfriend Luke took her to the first appointment, and the doctor listened carefully to her and her needs. He prescribed physical therapy and gave her the medication Ritalin for her attention deficits and slow processing speed. The physical therapy began to help her recover her movements and walking. She was still unable to drive and could not ambulate well due to dizziness. She went through the services of the physical therapist but eventually was discharged.

Jessica was incredibly determined as a student in psychology. She was used to getting straight A's, and she decided to return to school in the fall semester and take one class in addition to practicum which was twenty hours of counseling in an adjacent town, which was forty-five minutes away. She slowly learned to drive again, but it was a long process. She felt greatly confident about her counseling skills in her very first practicum at a shelter for women and children who had been abused. I was proud of her ability to have such a rigorous schedule so soon, but she seemed like a natural counselor. She obtained many accolades from her supervisors, which helped boost her self-esteem, even though she still had many cognitive issues that plagued her, such as slow processing speed and inattention. She often came to me for advice about how to work with her clients. I was happy to share my knowledge with her and was enormously proud that she was able to take on such a big project at this stage of her recovery. She also took one academic class.

Jessica became extremely frustrated when writing a paper. It usually took her two or three days to write a perfect a paper and receive a high A on it. This time, it took her three times the usual amount of time to complete the paper, and she received a B on it. That was not OK in her book, and she realized that although she was receiving academic accommodations through a 504 plan at the University, she needed to go to a rehabilitation program. I researched the programs, and we all decided upon the program. It was awfully expensive, but she needed it and it was a comprehensive program with speech therapy, occupational therapy, physical therapy, and neuropsychology.

Luke was her dedicated driver, and he drove her forty-five minutes to the clinic, starting at 9:00 a.m. He went back to pick her up at 3:00 p.m. He put his life on hold to make sure she went to her rehabilitation program each day. She started to make remarkable progress and found that the physical therapy she received was especially helpful for her dizziness as well as her overall stamina. She asked the physical therapist if she could run more on the treadmill and was told she could. Jessica was the first patient to ever ask to do more. She told her neurologist about the positive effects of exercise, and an intern that was in the room with them confirmed that he was studying the positive effects of exercise on TBI and it was found to be amazingly effective.

The rehabilitation program helped Jessica feel like she was able to do something to help herself get better. She commented that her skills were not as impaired as some of the other patients. She worked extremely hard and took her rehabilitation very seriously. She always did her PT homework and placed it on the refrigerator as a reminder to do it. I was so proud of my precious daughter. She worked so hard every day in that program! Her boyfriend was always at her side and took off the fall semester from school to be her caretaker and helper. She decided to enroll in counseling, which was helpful for her emotional self-control. Despite some difficult moments, Luke and I saw her begin to heal slowly but continuously.

> "Let us not become weary in doing good, for at the proper time we will reap a harvest if we do not give up." (Gal. 6:9)

I was so thankful to God for her healing. Although it was not a sudden and immediate event, I saw God's hand in her healing, which took place in baby steps each day. Her words came to her more easily, and her ability to complete her schoolwork also improved. She took her medication when she had to be attentive in class or during her practicum. It really helped her get through some difficult times, but she knew it was only temporary. I was so impressed how she worked so diligently with the goal of becoming more self-sufficient and doing the best she could possibly do.

Jessica also found healing from her pet dog Buddy. The dog was an extremely sweet Huskey that was her companion and emotional support animal. Buddy was always a sweet and happy dog, and I know that having her around to help Jessica recover was also an especially important part of her healing.

About a year after her accident, she began experiencing PTSD symptoms in which she remembered the moment of the accident. She had panic attacks and great difficulty with these intrusive memories. Slowly, with help from her boyfriend and me, she overcame them. She used the coping skills she had learned in counseling, and I believe that the prayers that were sent up for her also helped heal her trauma.

> "If you remain in me and my words
> remain in you, ask whatever you wish,
> and it will be done for you." (John 15:7)

Day by day, Jessica improved in her cognitive functioning and overall health. She slowly weaned off her Ritalin medication because she did not need it anymore. She was receiving accolades from her professors at her graduate school and was making A's in all her classes. Her thesis was accepted to be presented at the American Psychological Association in Washington DC! Jessica graduated with her master's degree in counseling psychology with all A's and one B. She took the Graduate Record Exam and received a score in the 90th percentile nationally! This was such a blessing because it was direct data that proved her cognitive skills were better than average; she was back to her amazing self with all the skills and abilities she had prior to her accident.

Her face is so beautiful now, not a scar in sight at all. Her eyebrow grew back perfectly. Even the scars on her arms and legs have healed. There is a slight discoloration on her knees, but other than that, she is extremely beautiful, and she looks as if she never had an accident that marred her face. She is picture perfect and is beautiful inside and out.

There is no doubt in my mind that God allowed this accident to happen. She asked me one day, "Mom, do you think God saved me so I could help other people through counseling?" I told her yes, it was highly likely. I was so happy to hear that she felt in some way that God was helping her with her healing. Her faith is different than mine. I am much more active in my faith, and she is more private. However, I know beyond a shadow of a doubt that God allowed her to beat the odds, and He healed her brain, her body, and her emotions.

We still have a few rough moments, but my daughter, my love of my life, is back, and she is ready to do big and wonderful things for others. She is in the process of applying to schools to obtain her doctorate degree in psychology. She wants to help others who are struggling, especially children. I am so proud of the woman she has become and that God anointed us both before her accident and carried us through all the rough and difficult bumps in the road that took about two years to navigate.

I am convinced that the medical evidence in her case supports that her healing was a miracle. Sometimes God shows us a miracle just because He can or that we ask. He is an amazing God, full of love and grace. We simply need to keep our minds and hearts open and understand that something bad can be turned into something good if we let God guide us through it! We also need to know that through our suffering, God does not leave our side and that there is beauty in suffering because it causes us to grow in our faith and know God more intimately.

> "But for you who revere my name, the sun of righteousness will rise with healing in its rays. And you will go out and frolic like well-fed calves." (Mal. 4:2)

The Perseverance that Comes from God

My niece Alisha was a bubbly, sweet and intelligent girl from the time she came to this earth. She always had a smile on her face, was a lover of animals, a gifted artist, and a kind and wonderful child.

When she was in high school, her father tragically died from alcoholism and a heroin over dose. Her father was not a drug user, but he drank heavily. He asked Alicia the day before he died if she would scuba dive with him. She declined his offer because he was drunk. Later the next day, a call came from the police and Alicia's father had died from a one-time use of heroin. He was an alcoholic but not a drug user, but the police informed my sister's family that a bad batch of heroine had circulated the town and had left many dead in its wake.

This event was devasting to my niece Alisha and her family. It was such a sad and horrible event that shook our family, but especially my two nieces. Alisha was unable to talk about her feelings, so she kept them inside and tried to appear as if everything was fine. She was miserable inside, torn with grief, guilt, and depression. The thought that if only she had gone scuba diving with him, was a "what if" scenario that ran through her head.

Later during her high school years, it was discovered that she was hooked on opioids. She was coming off the drugs and was going into withdrawals, and my sister quickly found a rehabilitation hospital. She spent the required time there, and was set up with aftercare services. Alicia stayed clean for a while, but relapsed many times. She was jailed at one point for going down the interstate in her car in the wrong direction drunk and high and hit an ambulance. She started shooting up heroin and other drugs. My sister had her in rehabilitation programs numerous times—too many to count. My sister never gave up on her and tried desperately to find a way to heal her broken heart and heal her addiction, which is a disease in and of itself. Despite the excellent intervention, Alicia could not stay clean. She deteriorated to the point that she was homeless.

Shortly after Alicia lost contact with her family, I came to my sister's house for a family wedding. My sister said that Alicia was homeless, wandering the streets in her slippers with no coat and no car or cell phone. My sister was hysterical, wanting to get in touch with her daughter. She found out about Alicia's situation from an acquaintance who did not know her whereabouts at the time I arrived at my sister's house. I sprang into immediate action and told my sister, "We need to pray for her to call you within four hours." I knew I had to be very specific because every minute she was gone and missing increased the possibility she could overdose and die.

I grabbed my sister's hands and prayed a mother's prayer, asking Jesus to find her immediately, give her the means to call home, and call her mother within four hours. Within two hours, my sister received a call from an unknown number. On the other line was her daughter Alicia! We praised Jesus for answered prayers and also for looking out after Alicia. Even if Alicia did not feel His presence at that time, He was with her through all of her drug-using episodes of shooting up, using dirty needles, and hanging out in crack houses. My sister quickly called around and found a sober house for Alicia to live for a while.

> "In the same way, the Spirit helps us in our weakness. We do not know what we ought to pray for, but the Spirit himself intercedes for us through wordless groans. And he who searches our hearts knows the mind of the Spirit, because the Spirit intercedes for God's people in accordance with the will of God." (Rom. 8:26–27)

My sister and I had a sigh of relief, but we both knew that the disease of addiction was a powerful tool often used by the enemy Satan. Although this is a disease that many blame the addict, it is a true addiction that is not just a series of bad choices. Substance abuse changes the brain in many terrible and physical ways, making the addict less able to say no. It's also a way to mitigate emotional pain, and it becomes a driving force that one cannot control. It's like riding on a roller coaster, except there is no one at the controls. It's complete and total chaos for the addict, his/her family, and others. Most addiction counselors acknowledge that it takes an average of ten rehabilitation treatments before an addict becomes clean for good. Many do not make it and die before they are healed.

Alicia reentered another sober house after her relapse in the summer. She met a friend who had a small child, three years old. They were celebrating his third birthday, and she walked into the room when they were blowing out the candle on his cupcake. That situation opened her eyes, and she realized at that moment she wanted a new start. However, she needed to work hard and stay clean. She found a job and worked diligently. She had dropped out of college due to her addiction and had no special job training or skills. However, she was a hard worker, and her work ethic helped her stay employed.

Alicia had to fight the craving of doing drugs every minute of the day. Just like the folks from Alcoholics Anonymous say, "One day at a time." That was a motto she endorsed, but it was difficult.

A few months passed and it was Thanksgiving. My sister, Alicia's mother always hosted Thanksgiving at her house. We were all there at my sister's house: my entire family, Alicia, and her new friend and son. It was great to see Alicia but I could still see the stress and sadness in her eyes, despite being sober for the last few months.

My sister knew of my spiritual gifts and immediately asked me to do intercessory prayer over Alicia. I was so excited and happy to find out after speaking with Alicia that she was more than ready for that experience; she was beaming with excitement. She didn't really know what intercessory prayer entailed, but she felt loved that many around her wanted to do it.

> "Is anyone among you sick? Let them call the elders of the church to pray over them and anoint them with oil in the name of the Lord. And the prayer offered in faith will make the sick person well; the Lord will raise them up. If they have sinned, they will be forgiven. Therefore, confess your sins to each other and pray for each other so that you may be healed. The prayer of a righteous person is powerful and effective." (James 5:14-16)

We went into my sister's bedroom and shut the door. I asked Alicia to sit down in the chair. I was present, along with my sister and Alicia's close friend. I used blessed oil and anointed her hands and forehead. I asked her want she wanted from Jesus, and she said to be healed. My sister, her friend, and I all were touching her. I turned to Jesus and began praising Him, praising God, and asking the Holy Spirit to descend upon us. I prayed exactly what the Holy

Spirit told me to say, word for word. I asked for Jesus to heal her addiction and to heal her emotionally, spiritually, physically, and in every way possible. I noticed a very strong warm sensation on my hands. I looked at Alicia, and she was crying soft tears but was sweating profusely. It was the middle of winter, and I literally saw sweat running down her face and her arms. Her hands and body were also hot, and the heat literally radiated from her body.

The prayer lasted a while, but I did not know the time frame. All I know is that Jesus was healing her and cleansing her. The heat was a manifestation of the Holy Spirit that I often see when He heals others through me. I am simply a conduit, an instrument of healing on this earth that Jesus uses through the Holy Spirit.

After I finished praying, she said that the experience was incredible. She felt an incredible peace but also love. She acknowledged the intense heat, but did not know why it happened. I thanked Jesus for healing her, and I told her to claim that she was healed and to thank Jesus for healing her. She did claim it and thanked Jesus. I also felt intense heat, emotional crying, and an amazing sense of love and peace. Whenever Jesus and the Holy Spirit come together for a healing, the person has to be open and believe that a healing is possible. If they are angry at someone or themselves, or don't really believe it's possible, the healing many not happen.

"If you believe, you will receive whatever you ask for in prayer." (Matt. 21:22)

In the following months I saw that Alicia was flourishing. She had her sweet, bubbly personality back. Alicia told her mother that after the prayer, God took her desire to do drugs away. It was gone completely. There were no cravings; they just left her. Her path to wellness involved perseverance, but God gave that to her. She had to work hard to stay on the right path, but there was no doubt in her mind that the day she was prayed over, she was healed by Jesus Christ.

She is enrolled in college and wants to be a counselor for those who are addicted to drugs and alcohol. Alicia has a purpose in her life, a new direction, and a new peace. God does not judge or admonish drug addicts. They are His children, and He desires their healing from drugs or alcohol as much as others who have physical diseases. Jesus loves to heal others, and He can heal addicts. When Jesus is present in the life of a former addict, His peace that passes understanding is present and alive. Satan can no longer use deception and drugs as a way to steer individuals away from God when they accept divine healing and His loving presence in their hearts.

> "Finally, be strong in the Lord and in his mighty power. Put on the full armor of God, so that you can take your stand against the devil's schemes. For our struggle is not against flesh and blood, but against the rulers, against the authorities, against the powers of this

dark world and against the spiritual forces of evil in the heavenly realms. Therefore put on the full armor of God, so that when the day of evil comes, you may be able to stand your ground, and after you have done everything, to stand. Stand firm then, with the belt of truth buckled around your waist, with the breastplate of righteousness in place, and with your feet fitted with the readiness that comes from the gospel of peace. In addition to all this, take up the shield of faith, with which you can extinguish all the flaming arrows of the evil one. Take the helmet of salvation and the sword of the Spirit, which is the word of God." (Eph. 6:10-17)

When I asked what Alicia felt about her experience four years later, she revealed that she indeed acknowledged that she was healed by Jesus. She related that He brought her the perseverance to stay on the right track, the perseverance that can only come from a divine place.

Christina's Message from God

January 2021

The writing of this book took place because God spoke relentlessly to me and then to Leah to do it. His hand guided every word. He let me know that many people would be blessed by the message, and many would come to know Him or return to Him because of it. I felt humbled and happy that God asked me to take part in such a project.

I also began reflecting on the reason for our suffering. At the time of this writing, my previous father-in-law was sick with COVID and in the hospital in Italy. I prayed and prayed for his recovery, but he did not make it and passed away the first part of January 2021. My children were devastated to lose their beloved grandfather who was truly an amazing man. At the same time, my youngest son was also diagnosed with COVID and was extremely ill. He is still recovering and has not yet been released from medical care. He had severe pneumonia, along with other serious symptoms. At the time of this writing, he is still recovering.

I was also praying relentlessly for my aunt Glenda who had stage four breast cancer over the end of December 2020 and into the beginning of January 2021. She battled it for several years, but when the medical team found it had spread throughout her body, they stopped treatment. She passed away just after my children's grandfather died the second week of January 2021. During this time, my eighty-seven-year-old mother was trying to get ready to travel to Iowa to say her goodbyes to my aunt (her sister). In the process of getting ready to go on the trip she fell and suffered a terrible traumatic brain injury with brain bleeding. My family and friends prayed, and she was able to return home after two days in the hospital, but with a lot of rehabilitation therapy that was needed. I also had a dear friend lose his second brother in death from cancer at this time. This meant that two brothers died at different times, the last one very recently.

I began to wonder why God allowed suffering of good people and why certain people did not live, despite the prayers that were sent up to heaven to our heavenly Father. I began to reflect and pray and realized that there was meaning that sprung from suffering and death; and turning it to God allowed terrible events to have a silver lining and even become miracles. If the way I prayed was not answered in the way I desired, I learned that God did answer my prayers perfectly. Trusting in Jesus is the answer in good times and in bad.

I now understand that many that are sick, or wounded are not healed on this earth. However, Earth is not our true home, and those that are taken to paradise in heaven do not have a "poor outcome." It is beauty in itself because sometimes even grief can bless our lives in ways never imagined, and it reminds us that we will see them again when we go to our true home, heaven. Sometimes we get so attached to this world we forget that this is just a very temporary place, this earth we live on. We are here to learn messages of love, mercy and forgiveness—and to trust God in times of darkness, in fact, in all circumstances. This is because our minds are not as vast as God's, and we simply do not have the understanding to grasp why these things happen to some but not others. I learned that I must let go of those who die. God transitions them to heaven, our true home. Love is forever, and I simply love them differently. I believe they can look down upon us from heaven, and that thought gives me great comfort.

When miracles on earth happen, we must remember who performed them; it is God, His son Jesus, and the Holy Spirit. Nothing happens in this earth that does not pass by God first. Therefore, trusting in Him is vital to keeping our faith alive and knowing that good can come out of our grief, trials, and sorrow.

My habit when I drive to work is to listen to praise music. One day while driving, I heard the song "Blessings," by Laura Story. I felt intense heat and a tingling that the Holy Spirit was with me. I also felt that God wanted the lyrics of this song included in this book. The message of the song was a similar message as our book: tragedy or difficult times can teach us lessons and bring us closer to God.

The song won a Grammy and was certified gold by the Recording Industry Association of America (RIAA).

The following lyrics are quoted with permission from the song writer who also has an amazing ministry with books, music, and inspirational talks. Please refer to https://laurastorymusic.com/ for more information on her speaking tour, books, and music.

Laura Story Lyrics

"Blessings"

We pray for blessings, we pray for peace
Comfort for family, protection while we sleep
We pray for healing, for prosperity
We pray for Your mighty hand to ease our suffering
And all the while, You hear each spoken need
Yet love us way too much to give us lesser things

Cause what if Your blessings come through raindrops
What if Your healing comes through tears
What if a thousand sleepless nights are what it takes to know You're near
What if trials of this life are Your mercies in disguise

We pray for wisdom, Your voice to hear
We cry in anger when we cannot feel You near
We doubt Your goodness, we doubt Your love

As if every promise from Your word is not enough
And all the while, You hear each desperate plea
And long that we'd have faith to believe

Cause what if Your blessings come through raindrops
What if Your healing comes through tears
What if a thousand sleepless nights are what it takes to
know You're near
What if trials of this life are Your mercies in disguise

When friends betray us
When darkness seems to win
We know the pain reminds this heart
That this is not
This is not our home

It's not our home

Cause what if Your blessings come through raindrops
What if Your healing comes through tears
And what if a thousand sleepless nights are what it takes
to know You're near

What if my greatest disappointments or the aching
of this life
Is the revealing of a greater thirst this world can't satisfy
And what if trials of this life-
The rain, the storms, the hardest nights
Are Your mercies in disguise

Acknowledgements

Acknowledgments from Christina

This book would not be possible without the understanding of how to use the gifts God bestowed upon me through the Holy Spirit, so I want to thank Him for choosing both Leah and me for this project before we incarnated to this earth. Next, I want to thank my wonderful husband for his love, support, encouragement, and his guidance and reminders to always stay humble. I want to thank my daughter and my niece for allowing me to be a part of their healing journeys.

I want to thank Xulon Press for all their assistance and guidance in this project that was led by God's hand. Finally, I want to acknowledge the Charismatic prayer group that helped me understand how to understand my spiritual gifts and use them to glorify God and help others. Their love, support and guidance taught me how to listen for God's words through the Holy Spirit which has helped my faith grow immensely, and it continues to grow each and every day.

Acknowledgments from Leah

There are many people to thank for helping with this book. My husband, Nick, was my computer guy. My granddaughter, Mackenzie "Kenzie," helped with the paintings for the book. The rest of the family helped with words of encouragement and prayers. Thanks to all at Xulon Press for all their help and guidance. A special thanks to God the Father, Jesus the Son, and the Holy Spirit for their love and inspiration.

Special acknowledgements and thanks from the authors

A special thanks and tribute to Jamie Arevalo for the cover photograph of the book. Without his supportive direction we would not have such a breathtaking photograph of God's creation.

We thank Christie Owens for her talents in creating such a beautiful picture of God's loving glory.

For our dear friend, Courtney Adams, we thank God for you each day and are thankful to have you as our chosen family. You perfectly captured the joy we had in writing this for the Lord.

A special thank you to Leah's granddaughter, Mackenzie, in all her painting and computer work!

Illustration Credits

The Trinity Cross done in resin and painted by
Nick Bickel

"Duck in Flight" painted in oil by Leah Bickel

"House in the Country" painted in oil by Leah Bickel

"Fruit of the Vine" painted in acrylic by
Mackenzie Reynolds

"Bumblebee in Flight" painted in acrylic by
Mackenzie Reynolds

"Winter scene" painted in oil by Leah Bickel

"Morning Glories" painted in acrylic on wood by
Leah Bickel

"Ichthys (Fish)" painted in acrylic by Mackenzie Reynolds

"Flowers" painted in acrylic by Mackenzie Reynolds

"Harvest Corn" painted in acrylic on wood by Leah Bickel

"Mother and child" painted in oil by Leah Bickel

Back Cover painting by Christie Owens

About the Authors

C hristina Della Nebbia-Arevalo grew up in Iowa in a loving, Christian home. She was raised in the Methodist Church and converted to the Catholic faith 23 years ago. She is a licensed psychologist and works in private practice. After witnessing the miracle healings of herself, her daughter, and her friend Leah, the book was written. Christina is married to Jamie Arevalo, and they live in the Dallas Fort-Worth metroplex. They enjoy playing tennis together, working out, traveling, and cooking together. Christina and her husband enjoy spending time with their children and grandchildren who are the joy of their lives.

Leah and her husband retired to northwest Mississippi in 2017. They moved back home from the Dallas, Texas, area. Leah was raised Baptist and started hearing the voice of God as a child, and the intimacy with God grew as she grew in her faith. She came into the Catholic Church when she married her husband in 1973, which was a difficult decision for her. She prayed diligently and felt God wanted her to become Catholic and worship with her husband. Thus, she began a new journey in Christ. In 2002, she and her husband joined a charismatic prayer group, and they both were blessed. They both came to a deeper understanding as they walked in the Spirit of God. Leah retired from nursing in the early 1990's, opened her own business, and then retired from it in 2016.

CPSIA information can be obtained
at www.ICGtesting.com
Printed in the USA
BVHW090009280721
613015BV00023B/841